# SHOULD
# I STAY

— or —

# *Should*
# *I Go?*

# SHOULD I STAY

# or

# *Should I Go?*

A FINANCIAL ADVISOR'S GUIDE TO THINKING
THROUGH THEIR BIGGEST DECISION

## Mindy Diamond

FOUNDER AND CEO OF DIAMOND CONSULTANTS

Diamond Consultants
marketing@diamond-consultants.com
36 Cattano Avenue
Morristown, NJ 07960

*Should I Stay or Should I Go?*, Mindy Diamond—first edition
ISBN 978-1-955242-59-2

# Early Praise for
## *Should I Stay or Should I Go?*

"*I've worked with Mindy for over twenty years. She is knowledgeable about the business, pays attention to the details, and does the right thing. Most importantly, she cares about her clients and wants them to succeed. It's no surprise she's written a book focused on helping advisors.*"

**Barry Sommers**
*CEO,* Wells Fargo Wealth & Investment Management

"*One of the most pivotal decisions an advisor will ever make is deciding who to partner with and how that working relationship will forever alter the future of their business and their life. In* Should I Stay or Should I Go?, *Mindy Diamond masterfully combs through the complexity of this life-altering decision and provides advisors with a clear game plan of how to detangle themselves from the most important decision they will ever make—for the sake of their clients, their families, and their legacy.*"

**Ron Carson**
*Founder and CEO,* Carson Group

*"Every financial advisor who cares deeply about their clients should read this book. Mindy has written a comprehensive guide to determining the ideal place to serve your clients, now and in the future.* Should I Stay or Should I Go? *explores all of the available options in our industry with useful frameworks to help you think through this critical process."*

**Jerry Davidse, CFP®**
*CEO,* Presilium Private Wealth
(Former Merrill advisor)

*"Mindy was early to recognize that many of the best advisors in our industry are looking to challenge the status quo. No one understands the spectrum of choices better than her, and she lays it all out right here. Every financial advisor in the country should read this book!"*

**Vince Fertitta**
*President,* Sanctuary Wealth
(Former Merrill leader)

*"Since founding Diamond Consultants twenty-five years ago, Mindy Diamond has been a key player in the evolving wealth advisory ecosystem. In this book, she helps advisors define their 'why' they may consider making a change. There are two big 'Es' when considering a move, Economics and Emotions. This book is a brilliant framework to manage and balance both for your best possible business future."*

**Matthew B. Cooper**
*President,* Beacon Pointe Advisors

*"If not for the expert guidance I received from Mindy and Louis Diamond, I'm not sure I would have landed exactly where I am today. It was Mindy's podcast that first opened my eyes to the real potential outside of Merrill and served as the catalyst to begin asking myself the tough questions. But it was Diamond Consultants' process that guided me down paths I would not have considered. The book serves as solid proof that they know their stuff—and it works!"*

**Michael Henley, CFP®, CPWA®, CRPC®, RMA®**
*Founder & CEO and Private Wealth Advisor,*
Brandywine Oak Private Wealth
(Former Merrill advisor)


*"I first met Mindy Diamond a few decades ago, and, within minutes, I realized this was not just another recruiter with a passing interest in independent wealth management. Over the years that followed, she has distinguished herself as a thought leader intent on educating advisors about a career path that is more rewarding but, admittedly more arduous, than just taking a check and going to another firm. The wealth management space has seen unprecedented expansion and, with that, brings new complexities.* Should I Stay or Should I Go? *is a long-overdue companion guide for evaluating the myriad of options that are now available to financial advisors and finding a path that resonates with the advisor's true self."*

**Brian Hamburger**
*President & CEO,* MarketCounsel Consulting
*Chief Counsel,* The Hamburger Law Firm

*"As a thirty-one-year veteran and a Barron's Top 100 advisor, one of the first things you embrace is: 'time is money.' After having made several broker dealer changes in my career, I would have given anything to have known about this book or Mindy Diamond's team and the excellent work they do. Instead, I wasted precious time doing my own due diligence. Don't make that same mistake. Read this book and call the experts at Diamond Consultants!"*

**Erin Botsford**
*Founder, CEO, Creator,*
The Elite Advisor Success System™

*"Changing firms is a big decision for the leaders of wealth management practices. Navigating the intricacies of that decision is often best supported by a trusted river guide. In our industry there is one such guide that stands above the rest: Mindy Diamond. And in true Mindy Diamond fashion, she has crafted a reference guide for advisors that is thoughtful, accessible, structured, and logical—and starts and ends with helping advisors both support their clients and live their best business lives. Advisors contemplating such a journey should start with Should I Stay or Should I Go?—period."*

**Rich Steinmeier**
*Divisional President,* LPL Financial

*"The key to unlocking the highest levels of success as a financial advisor comes from being hyper-intentional about every aspect of your practice. This is especially true of where you call your (financial) home. In this book, Mindy has again demonstrated that she and her team are the absolute best at helping advisors find the best home for their practice and their clients. Every advisor, from Wire, to IBD, to RIA needs to read this book, answer the tough questions it asks, and then act on the results."*

**Matthew Jarvis, CFP®**
The Perfect RIA | Jarvis Financial Services


*"As a former wirehouse advisor (most recently UBS) who built a $5B business in the brokerage world, I recognize the value of challenging one's goals versus that of their firm. In this book, Mindy offers a strategic thought process that equips advisors with the tools to ask the right questions, think critically, and objectively evaluate their current situation. Whether contemplating a change or not,* Should I Stay or Should I Go? *is a comprehensive guide that encourages self-reflection, walking advisors through a thoughtful process of professional self-discovery. Mindy and her team are one of the best in the business—and this book provides a glimpse into the unique care they put into every advisor relationship and transition."*

**Robert Sechan**
*CEO, Cofounder,* NewEdge Wealth
*Comanaging Partner,* NewEdge Capital Group
(Former UBS advisor)

"I wish I had read this in early 2020 as we began our own due diligence process. Mindy Diamond has created a step-by-step guide to determining whether the firm you are with, and the business model you are in, provides your clients with the best possible wealth management experience. Read this book if you want to be a better financial advisor. It will expose you to the vast array of business models and practice options that are available to today's financial advisor."

**Kelly Milligan, CPWA®, CRPC®, C(k)P®, CPFA**
*Managing Partner,* Quorum Private Wealth
(Former Merrill advisor)

"It's about time someone accepted the challenge of writing a book about the complex landscape surrounding financial advisors thinking about new opportunities and the even more complex process of thoroughly considering their options from both a personal and professional perspective. For those who know Mindy Diamond, it's no surprise that she accepted the challenge. She has the rare, almost unique, combination of experience, insight, and extreme expertise that make this book a must-read for any financial advisor interested in something beyond the status quo."

**Michael Nathanson**
*CEO,* The Colony Group

*"Mindy provides an in-depth framework for self-assessment that every client-centric advisor must read! She shares her decades of experience and empathetic approach to helping advisors evaluate their options at a time when our industry is experiencing incredible change. It's a comprehensive 'how-to' that will help advisors truly evaluate their options."*

**Jack B. Petersen**
*Cofounder, Managing Partner,* Summit Trail Advisors
(Former Barclays Wealth advisor)


*"Mindy is a genuine industry titan. You'd be hard-pressed to find someone who, over the years, has played a more transformative role in helping advisors appreciate and then unlock their value in the marketplace. Whether you are a seasoned advisor contemplating a leap of faith or an aspiring professional seeking guidance, this book offers invaluable insights and practical advice to help you navigate the path to independence."*

**Robert (Rory) J. O'Hara III, CFP®, CRPC®**
*Founder & Senior Managing Partner,* Ausperity Private Wealth
(Former Merrill advisor)

# Dedication/Acknowledgement

To my team at Diamond Consultants, many of whom put their faith in me as their leader in the earliest of days. They are the very best there is—smart, talented, dedicated people with integrity beyond measure. I would be nowhere without them. And to my husband, Howard. My forever champion, cheerleader, and the love of my life.

# CONTENTS

# Resources

The tools and resources mentioned in this book are available for download via the QR code below or at https://www.diamond-consultants.com/book-resources/.

# Foreword

by Craig N. Robson, CFP®, CIMA®, CDFA®
Founding Principal and Managing Director,
Regent Peak Wealth Advisors

# My Search for Professional Happiness

It was a Thursday evening in November 2017 when I received an unsolicited call from Mindy Diamond. That call was the turning point in my diligence process.

As an advisor who had built his practice at Merrill Lynch cold calling (primarily from 1994 to 1999), I have a special affinity for anyone who has the courage to contact someone they don't know over the phone to offer services. At the time of Mindy's call, I was in the early stages of exploration, somewhat overwhelmed, and lacked direction in my journey toward professional happiness.

As an individual who recently built a custom home, I know how critical it is to have a competent team of professionals (builder, architect, designer) to help execute the plan. Analogous to that process, I lacked a team of experts and resources to guide me throughout my diligence journey to my final decision.

After my initial conversation with Mindy, I decided that she and her firm, Diamond Consultants, would be the best at representing me moving forward. Over the next few months, we modified my overall diligence process and developed clarity and efficiency, which resulted in me finalizing my decision in April 2018.

Unfortunately, due to unexpected family matters, I had to delay my transition date by approximately thirteen months. Yet the foundation had been set to seamlessly pick up the process in February 2019. By May 2019, I launched Regent Peak Wealth Advisors, LLC, and my search for professional happiness was complete.

When Louis Diamond recently asked me if I would be willing to write a foreword for their book, I asked about the topic and their intended audience. Upon reading *Should I Stay or Should I Go?*, I found myself wishing it had been available back in 2017. It's an ideal playbook for any advisor considering change—a process that Mindy and her team developed and perfected and which they are now making available to all advisors.

Reflecting on my pre-transition diligence and the process Mindy guided me through, I recall critical elements I feel an advisor should have in place and themes to identify to improve the potential for a successful transition.

While you may read some similar themes within this book, please know that these are my own experiences and thoughts.

1. **Take inventory of your personal situation.**
   On my resignation day, I was fifty years old and had just celebrated my twenty-fifth anniversary at the same firm. I cannot tell you how many times people looked at me

awkwardly when I told them I had worked for the same company since 1994, and I was planning on creating my own firm. A question you must ask yourself: Do you have the personal drive, health, support (family and friends), and financial resources to weather a transition? Look, I have yet to hear anyone acknowledge that they had an unsuccessful transition, yet they are out there. Diamond Consultants and I had some honest discussions about these topics and more. You owe it to yourself, your clients, and your team to understand the commitment needed to successfully execute any transition.

2. **Find an objective sounding board.**
Identify individuals or entities who have your best interests at heart and who won't tell you what you want to hear but what you need to hear. I engaged both an executive coach and Diamond Consultants to help me throughout the various decision points. Mindy and her team were the proverbial knowledge resource. They helped me understand the overall wealth management landscape (wirehouse, regional firms, independent broker dealers, banks, registered independent advisors, hybrid offerings, etc.) and how to differentiate through the various offers we were receiving.

3. **Include your team in the process.**
One of the early questions Mindy asked me was if I had shared with my team my decision to explore options specific to a transition. My personal view was that our team was stronger together and that I owed it to each of them to disclose my thoughts and see if they were interested in joining me. We were all frustrated and felt that

professionally we, and our clients, were being limited by our previous employer (you may hear the term "optionality" in your diligence process). Mindy and her team helped me communicate to my team the most salient points related to this process and guided me toward effective ways to include them so that when it came time to finalize my decision, they were well informed of the various choices for consideration.

4. **Focus on your top three to five goals and priorities to guide your decision.**
   Keep these as your North Star; this compass will direct you to your ultimate decision. The "Defining Your Best Business Life Self-Assessment" (only a subset of which is contained in this book) helped clarify my goals and get my non-negotiables onto paper. In looking back at my original list, here are some I documented: 1) Optionality to create our own values, as well as market and message our brand; 2) a firm that could be nimble and make quick decisions; 3) an environment and culture where our entire team could professionally and financially grow; 4) opportunities to source and provide investments and services to ultra-high-net-worth families; 5) collaboration with other actual fiduciaries (not those who claim they are) on behalf of the families we serve. As I kept referring to this list with Mindy and Louis, we collectively realized that the independent channel was the optimal choice for me and my team.

5. **Expect the unexpected.**
   I felt our team was more than prepared, and we were ready to transition. In fact, many resources we trust told us that

they hadn't seen a team this prepared. On a few occasions in my first year, Mindy or Louis and I would huddle up, and we would review our progress as well as our challenges. From these conversations, I always came away with suggestions to help me go forward. To this day, I still periodically contact them to help me with unexpected or unfamiliar situations.

In May of 2023, my team and I celebrated our fourth anniversary, and we are grateful that we decided to create our own firm.

# Preface

# An Invitation to Live Your Best Business Life

E very advisor strives for alignment between their professional goals and values on the one hand and the actual experience of work life on the other.

When you achieve alignment, you have all of this:

- Passion for the work you do.
- Agency over the decisions you make on behalf of your clients.
- The ability to act as a true fiduciary to clients.
- Freedom to spend your days feeling happy, productive, and valued.

The result of finding that congruence is the sweet spot that I call your "best business life."

As a financial advisor, you hold yourself to the highest standards of integrity, honesty, and credibility. You've been successful in your field because you take your professional responsibilities seriously. You're dedicated to your clients. And you've earned their trust. *But are you living your best business life?*

The good news for advisors is that the wealth management world has evolved at a pace far faster than in years past, creating a waterfall of possibilities unlike any you've seen before—and it seems to be growing and changing daily. This evolution has revealed an industry landscape with a plethora of options for advisors, offering varying degrees of freedom, flexibility, and control.

So it would seem that finding your best business life would be easy.

But with more options comes greater confusion—because to effectively assess these alternatives, you need to weigh them against many other factors, starting with your own goals.

It's time to embark on a journey to answer this question:

"Can I say, with absolute certainty, that where I am is still the best place for my clients and me?"

Uncovering the answer starts with asking yourself more probing questions. These will help you gain clarity on your goals and vision; identify the gaps between where you are and where you want to be; and challenge the status quo with courage, honesty, and real self-awareness.

My goal with this book is to provide a strategic thought process and road map to professional self-discovery. I aim to help you ask the right questions and to think critically and objectively about what your best business life looks like—and to help you weigh what's good about your current situation and the ties that bind you against the disruption and hassle that always go along with any change. Only then can you draw your own conclusion—with absolute certainty—that you are or are not in the ideal place for both you and your clients.

There are two things this book is not, however.

First and foremost, it is neither designed nor intended to push advisors into making a move. The mere fact that you are reading these pages indicates you have an interest in exploring not just the landscape, but also your own goals and vision for the future. This does not mean that you will change firms or models. In fact, you may read these pages and conclude, perhaps quickly, that your best choice is to stay right where you are because you've determined that your current situation meets your needs and ethical standards and enables you to do what's best for those you serve. And that's a wonderful outcome, because, even if you stay, the simple act of inquiry will broaden both your perspective and your confidence.

Secondly, this book is not a guide on *how to* transition from one firm to another, should you decide to do so, because the process and details of this are vastly different for each advisor, firm, or model. Certainly, it's something we'd be happy to help you with should you come to the conclusion that a move is in the best interests of yourself, your team, and your clients, but that is not the goal of this book.

Over the past two decades, I've helped countless advisors like you to examine their career options and have guided hundreds toward new firms and models. I've also counseled nearly as many to stay put, because, after going through the process outlined in this book, they determined that they were exactly where they needed to be. Ultimately, I helped each to embrace their best business lives.

But these advisors couldn't get to a final conclusion without answering this fundamental question: Should I stay or should I go?

So let's explore a process that will help you answer that very same question—and find the way to your best business life.

# Chapter One

# The Trapeze: Empowering Yourself to Let Go

As part of his 2009 book, *Warriors of the Heart: A Handbook for Conflict Resolution*,[1] author Danaan Perry wrote "The Parable of the Trapeze," in which he likened change to a series of trapeze swings:

> "Most of the time, I spend my life hanging on for dear life to my trapeze-bar-of-the-moment. It carries me along at a certain steady rate of swing and I have the feeling that I'm in control of my life…
>
> "But every once in a while as I'm merrily (or even not-so-merrily) swinging along, I look out ahead of me into the distance and what do I see? I see another trapeze bar swinging toward me. It's empty and I know, in that place in me that knows, that this new trapeze bar has my name on it. It is my next step, my growth, my aliveness coming to get me. In my heart of hearts I know that,

---

[1] Danaan Perry, *Warriors of the Heart: A Handbook for Conflict Resolution* (Bainbridge, Island, WA: Earthstewards Network, 2009).

for me to grow, I must release my grip on this present, well-known bar and move to the new one."

Have you ever been in a situation where you felt discontentment and were not sure why, or you knew you wanted to make a change, yet were uncomfortable or afraid of what the actual outcome might be? As a result, you allow momentum and even inertia to move you along, all the while trying to ignore the signs around you—harbingers of a changing environment—until you just can't avoid the signals and your own thoughts any longer.

I share this parable because it illustrates the emotional journey that anyone considering change goes through. I find it particularly relevant to advisors, because so many tell me that while they may not be wholly satisfied where they are, the thought of changing firms or models, or selling their business, is overwhelming, to say the very least.

Put another way, there's a great degree of discomfort, and even fear, attached to the unknown. That's why so many choose to hang on to the status quo, because there is familiarity there, despite the possibility that greater potential may await elsewhere.

Still, once you've seen that proverbial bar swinging toward you, it's impossible to unsee it—it just continues to beckon you.

Consider this: You're having a good year—annual revenue is up, you brought in a meaningful number of new clients, and you're living a balanced life that allows you to spend time with family and friends.

Yet there are things that just don't seem quite right.

- Complaints from support staff are increasing.
- You'd like to do things for clients that your firm won't allow you to deliver on.
- Attempts at marketing, self-branding, and differentiation are being thwarted by your firm's compliance directives.
- Getting told "no" too often is taking the fun out of the business and slowing you down.
- Your firm continues to tweak compensation, which makes you question the value you derive relative to the amount you're giving up.
- And, perhaps, most importantly, when you think about your future and the legacy you want to leave, you worry that you won't be able to maximize the value of the business you built and/or deliver excellence to clients.

At the same time, you may be watching as trusted colleagues leave their firms and join other traditional firms or launch their own—and the option of going independent piques your interest when you read the headlines announcing yet another business selling for an eye-popping multiple.

Why did others choose to reach out and grab that next trapeze bar while you continue to hold tight to the one you're on? How did they get the courage to let go and make the leap?

These folks didn't jump blindly from one bar to the next. They were empowered by knowledge.

The reality is that perhaps your view is limited or insular. Those who made the leap gained an expanded view of what their business life could be like beyond their current firm. They learned about the possibilities in a vastly evolved industry landscape. And having that knowledge gave them the courage and strength to make an educated decision on whether to hang on or choose to let go and reach for the next bar.

A greater understanding of what that swinging bar before you could represent would make the leap far less frightening.

> The goal is to gain greater agency over the decision of whether to hold on or let go.

But keep in mind that the goal of education isn't limited to inspiring you to reach for the next opportunity. Instead, it's to give you greater agency over the decision of whether to hold on or let go. It gives you permission to acknowledge that clinging to what may not be serving you and your clients best—perhaps out of fear, being overwhelmed, or sheer inertia—could be preventing you from moving forward.

Empowerment comes from gaining knowledge—after which you can give yourself permission to release your grip on the current bar to move on to the next one.

So let's get empowered!

# Chapter Two

# A Tour of the Evolved Industry Landscape

Typically, our conversations with advisors begin with an overview of the industry landscape. For many, it's enlightening—a reality check of how rapidly the industry continues to evolve. This background knowledge informs the self-assessment process that I will discuss in chapter three.

Let's take a step back to understand how the wealth management industry has evolved to its current state, with a series of transformative events in recent years, each of which spurred the growth and adaptation of firms and models:

The wild west brokerage culture of the 1980s and 1990s gave way to more of a fiduciary mindset at the turn of the millennium.

The brand distrust that developed as a result of the financial crisis in 2008 led to a validation of alternative models outside the major firms.

And, because of the COVID-19 pandemic, the evolution of the industry landscape accelerated, making advisors less reliant on branch infrastructure and more demanding of freedom and control.

The proliferation of change was propelled by visionary leaders and entrepreneurs who saw this changing advisor mindset as an opportunity. They perceived a gap between what advisors wanted and the traditional big brokerage firms' ability to fulfill those needs. This gave birth to new firms and affiliation models, each designed to directly address an updated set of criteria.

In the years prior to 2019, my firm, Diamond Consultants, would put together an annual white paper called "The Landscape of the Industry." Although it required a Herculean effort to create, it became outdated within a day of publishing.

Why? Because that's how fast the wealth management industry changes.

What remains relevant is the continuum in which we described the landscape. Essentially, envision a horizontal line that depicts the options in a series of model categories where a financial advisor may choose to practice.

This continuum[2] identifies every option from the most restrictive models (the biggest banks and brokerage firms) on the left to models offering the greatest amount of freedom and control (building a firm from scratch as an independent) on the right.

---

[2] Derived from "The Wealth Management Landscape Landscape at a Glance," available on the resources page at https://www.diamond-consultants.com/book-resources/.

**Figure 1. The Wealth Management Industry at a Glance by Diamond Consultants**

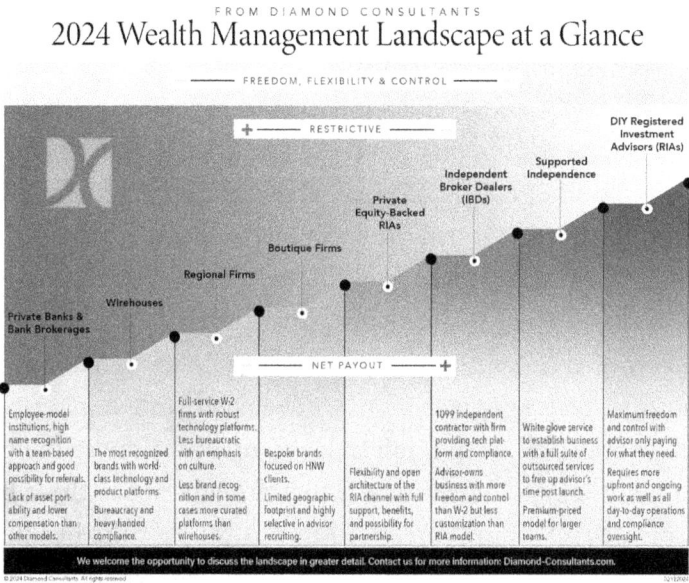

FROM DIAMOND CONSULTANTS
2024 Wealth Management Landscape at a Glance

While the explosive expansion of options is a good thing for advisors, their businesses, and clients, it's hard to gain clarity around the features and benefits of each model.

So let's unpack them from left to right.

## Private Banks and Bank Brokerages

Private banks tend to have real brand cachet and attract some of the most sophisticated wealth management talent in the industry. Firms like J.P. Morgan Private Bank, Bank of New York Mellon, and Citi Private Bank represent an interconnected, team-based approach where bankers, relationship managers, investors, and the like come together to service ultra-high-net-worth clients. While the salary-bonus compensation model of private banks may thwart entrepreneurial spirit, making it a model advisors often outgrow, many remain true to the banks they work for because they thrive on the certainty that comes with working at these large firms.

In the bank brokerage space, including the retail arms of Charles Schwab, Fidelity Investments, Chase, and Truist, advisors often sit in bank branches. They have less autonomy than those who practice in traditional private client groups because the bank believes it owns the clients; the advisors are usually restricted to a more limited overall platform.

While banks sometimes provide a built-in referral mechanism that drives growth, private bankers and bank branch advisors often tell us that referrals dry up over time as the bank attempts to place a governor on that growth. So, as these bank advisors become more interested in control over the businesses they've built, they often seek opportunities elsewhere.

While on the one hand, a bank model can be a great way to grow a business, the downside is that if an advisor chooses to change jerseys, bank assets that were originally referred to them are tied more closely to the bank and are harder to move. This makes it critical for bank advisors to determine whether they will ultimately stay or go as soon as possible, because the longer they work for the bank, the less portable their book will likely be.

As of this writing, as the competition for top talent has increased, most firms are more open than ever to recruiting private bankers and bank advisors provided they have largely portable books of business. A move can be more complicated because of the lack of Protocol[3] protection, but not impossible by any means. It's rare to see a bank advisor move 100 percent of their assets to a new firm or model, and it can often take longer than their nonbank peers for the assets to migrate. But provided that all parties' expectations are managed, we have seen many make these moves successfully.

## Wirehouse Firms

One step to the right on the continuum are the wirehouses, the most recognizable names in the wealth management space: Morgan Stanley Wealth Management, Merrill (a Bank of America Company), UBS Wealth Management, and Wells Fargo Advisors. These firms offer deep pockets, scale, and platforms that provide all-under-one-roof access to most everything needed to serve clients (including cutting-edge technology, robust investment platforms, lending, access to alternative investments, and trust capabilities). This allows them to offer a cradle-to-grave approach, starting with training programs for rookies and continuing on through attractive retire-in-place succession initiatives for tenured advisors.

Many advisors report that these firms manage to the lowest common denominator, a practice which limits risk to the firm by lowering the bar to accommodate the average advisor. Likewise, compliance oversight can be heavy-handed—as such,

---

[3] Smith Barney, Merrill Lynch, and UBS created the Protocol for Broker Recruiting in 2004 to stave off the common and expensive litigation that occurred when a departing advisor left one firm to join a competitor. Essentially, these firms agreed to a cease fire of sorts, permitting an advisor to freely leave one member firm and join another. As long as advisors adhered to the governing principles, they would be permitted to take a limited amount of client information and actively solicit these clients after moving to a new Protocol firm without fear of a temporary restraining order (TRO). In 2017, Morgan Stanley and UBS opted out of the Protocol. As of this writing, Wells Fargo and Merrill Lynch remain, along with more than 2,000 firms, as members of this seminal agreement.

when advisors opt to leave the wirehouse world, the number one driver is a desire for greater freedom and control. Surely, many advisors are now leaving big firms for boutiques or independence, but the remaining majority feel that, on par, life in an organization that "scaffolds" them is exactly what they want: The comfort of all-in-one-place access to best-in-class capabilities, stability, and a recognized brand name to match. And it's a formula that seems to work, as a recent Cerulli Associates report[4] indicated that wirehouse advisors are among the most productive in the industry.

In recent years, the wirehouses have been in and out of the recruiting game. While their leaders may abhor paying big transition deals to recruit top advisor talent, they recognize that the only way to remain relevant and beat the competition is to be aggressive. This means that transition packages being offered by the likes of Morgan, Merrill, UBS, and Wells have reached high watermarks—at least for now.

## Regional Firms

Another step to the right on the continuum are the regional firms. These firms have made a massive leap in recent years, shedding their long-held reputation of subpar leadership, technology, and platform. In the past decade, these W-2 models—such as Raymond James & Associates, RBC Wealth Management, Stifel, and Ameriprise Financial—recognized the opportunity to best their wirehouse counterparts. They turned the tables by hiring top leaders from the big brokerages and investing heavily in technology and platform. The result:

---

[4]  "Wirehouse Advisors Prove Their Worth by Measures of Productivity,"
    Cerulli Associates, February 7, 2022, https://www.cerulli.com/press-releases/
    wirehouse-advisors-prove-their-worth-by-measures-of-productivity.

An option for advisors who are seeking a culture rooted in the belief that the "advisor is client." As a result, advisors find the regionals to be less bureaucratic than their wirehouse counterparts; with direct access to senior management; nationwide footprints; and robust platforms, technology, and support. And the multichannel model, which exists at a number of regional firms (and provides the ability to join as an employee and shift to independence in the future), is attractive to many advisors who are thinking longer term.

Recently, regional firms have leveled the playing field by offering deals that are highly competitive and have more predictable compensation plans.

## Boutique Firms

After the financial crisis in 2008, firms in this category like Lehman Brothers, Bear Stearns, Barclays, and Credit Suisse were either absorbed by larger firms or disappeared entirely. This left a gaping hole in the industry landscape because these iconic firms had attracted sophisticated advisors who serviced high-net-worth clients and who wanted a more exclusive culture with many fewer advisors than their wirehouse counterparts.

As a result, in the past decade, smart leaders jumped in and filled the gap by creating or rebuilding models that would appeal to this constituency—a solid alternative to the big brokerage firms for these upper-echelon advisors. The boutique firms of yesteryear were replaced by the likes of Rockefeller Capital Management, J.P. Morgan Advisors, William Blair, and many more private equity-backed firms built on RIA infrastructure.

Because these boutique firms resonate with top advisors, they are experiencing great success recruiting talent. They provide a more intimate and collaborative culture built around a community of like-minded advisors, unique investment capabilities, and, in some cases, more creative, highly competitive transition deals.

## Independence

The independent models at the far-right end of the continuum offer the greatest amount of freedom, flexibility, and control. The ecosystem that arose to support independent advisors has matured rapidly over the past decade, solving challenges that had previously deterred entrepreneurial advisors who wanted the ability to run their own businesses. The result is a variety of options that provide varying degrees of support and transition capital.

### Private Equity-Backed RIAs

While registered investment advisors (RIAs) have employed financial advisors for decades, it wasn't until the last few years that top advisors considered joining RIAs as W-2 employees. Many advisors are attracted to the freedom, true open architecture, creativity, and culture of the independent space, yet covet the scaffolding and support of a traditional broker dealer. Private equity-backed RIAs have become a best-of-both-worlds option where advisors can tap into many of the benefits of independence, but also get a competitive recruitment deal and infrastructure.

While many RIAs may not offer any sort of recruitment deal, the firms most attractive to advisors will offer packages consisting of cash and equity. The latter is a true differentiator:

a wealth creation opportunity not offered in other captive channels.

Today, most RIAs recruiting advisors are backed by private equity sponsors, providing capital, deal-making expertise, and often creative deal structures allowing for capital gains tax benefit. These firms are of particular interest to high net worth- and ultra-high net worth-focused advisors. Examples of RIAs active in the recruitment of advisors are Steward Partners Global Advisory, Beacon Pointe Advisors, Cresset Capital, and IEQ Capital.

## Independent Broker Dealers (IBD)

The first of two subcategories in the independent space is the independent broker dealer (IBD) model, which includes firms like LPL Financial, Raymond James Financial, Wells Fargo Advisors Financial Network (FiNet), Ameriprise Financial, Commonwealth Financial Network, and Cambridge Investment Research—some of which also have employee models as previously referenced in the regional and wirehouse sections. These firms allow advisors to be business owners with the added benefit of back-office support and attractive transition deals. Historically, this model was ideal for an advisor with minimal fee-based business who was willing to give up some control in exchange for access to turnkey operations and support, as well as a curated platform and technology stack. Today, the IBD space attracts all kinds of advisors, even those with a significant amount of fee-based business who want a recruitment bonus package and more support than the RIA space might offer. Many IBDs are now multichannel, allowing an advisor to shift to RIA status while remaining under the firm's umbrella.

For better or worse, advisors who join an independent broker dealer are captive to the platform and compliance rules of the broker dealer.

## Supported Independence

In the years leading up to the early 2020s, the RIA space expanded to include a subcategory called supported independence. This has become one of the hottest models for advisors who have their sights set on becoming business owners, but don't want to deal with the headaches of initial setup (including acquiring real estate, managing office build-out, establishing legal entities, and creating a brand) and day-to-day middle- and back-office management. Instead, service providers—such as Dynasty Financial Partners, Sanctuary Wealth, NewEdge Advisors, and LPL Strategic Wealth Services—charge advisors a fee for the ability to off-load these tasks and leverage their platforms, technology, and thought leadership. In addition, many supported independent firms offer recruitment bonuses to reduce the risks of a move and defray start-up costs. They also offer liquidity solutions, which enable advisors to sell a minority stake in their practices.

Even within the supported independence category, choice abounds. Some models offer a centralized platform or shared ADV (a uniform form used by investment advisers to register with both the SEC and state securities authorities), while others assist advisors who endeavor to operate their own RIA.

## Registered Investment Advisors (RIA)

For those advisors seeking maximum control, there is the option to launch an independent firm as an RIA. These are comprised of fee-only RIAs and hybrid RIAs (for advisors who have a combination of fee-based and commissionable business). They can be do-it-yourselfers (DIYers) or those who leverage the services of a platform provider or consultants. The RIA space is defined by a truly open architecture—which means access to what we call the "whole of market." RIAs can "shop the Street" and create competition for price and service for virtually anything: lending, structured products, alternative investments, trust services, insurance, annuities, and everything in between. Assets are custodied with a third-party institutional custodian such as Schwab, Fidelity, and Pershing. Even LPL Financial, Raymond James, and Goldman Sachs have offerings to support registered investment advisors.

The RIA space is ideal for the advisor who wants to build an enterprise and eventually sell their business for top dollar, either by putting it up for bid on the open market or creating an internal sale or succession plan. Such businesses can grow via recruiting and acquisition, which can massively increase business value, a major driver for those looking to build something bigger. The RIA space may also be ideal for those who wish to run a fee-only practice today or in the future, as well as those who value having maximum control over all decision-making relative to their businesses.

Advisors who operate their own RIAs maximize payout and overall flexibility, but with the added responsibility of managing the start-up and ongoing business requirements.

## Recap

Armed with knowledge of the diverse options available in a greatly expanded landscape—a continuum from the most restrictive models (the biggest banks and brokerage firms) to those offering varying degrees of freedom and control (the independent space)—you have a new lens to view the possibilities. Next, let's develop some clarity on what drives you and what your goals are.

# Chapter Three

# Critical Questions You Should Ask Yourself

At Diamond Consultants, as we educate our advisor clients about the industry landscape, we guide them in parallel down a path of self-evaluation, helping them look honestly at themselves, their businesses, and their goals. Because every quality advisor believes they have a responsibility to be absolutely certain that everything they do will serve their clients' best interests, they use this self-evaluation to determine if their firm is in any way limiting or preventing them from doing their very best work.

To aid discovery, we designed a self-assessment to help you objectively appraise your current business life and gain clarity on whether where you are fully aligns with where you want to be now and in the future.

Ultimately, the answers will bring to light any incongruence that may exist and help better define your path forward.

All advisors should be regularly asking themselves these questions—regardless of whether they are considering a move or are perfectly content where they are—and they are a subset of a more extended appraisal we go through with our advisor clients.

Armed with an understanding of the waterfall of possibilities, you are now well-equipped to objectively evaluate your business life as it is today and gain clarity around what you envision for tomorrow. So, take the time to consider each of these fourteen questions (also available as a PDF on the resources page at https://www.diamond-consultants.com/book-resources/). Answer thoughtfully and honestly, as the responses will serve as the foundation for all the decisions that come next.

## Part One: Understanding the Impact of *Why* and *What* on Your Decision-Making Process

The first two questions ask you to dig deep into what sparks you most about the work that you do.

1. **As Simon Sinek suggests in his bestselling book, *Start With Why*, ask yourself *why* you are a financial advisor. What motivates you?**
   We ask this question first because many advisors lose sight of why they got into this line of work. Taking the time to remind yourself of your "why" can lead you back to your roots and create clarity around your goals.

2. **What aspects of your job as a financial advisor do you find most rewarding? (Check all that apply.)**
   Oftentimes advisors find themselves playing the role of a one-armed paper hanger—they get caught up in doing a wide variety of tasks that fall outside of their core competencies. Recognizing what you do best and what

feels most soulful to you will allow you to off-load those things that are better left to others. This is the foundation of building a profitable and long-lasting business that is scalable and destined for growth.

[   ] Managing client relationships
[   ] Prospecting
[   ] Financial planning
[   ] Investment management
[   ] Managing a team
[   ] Leading a business
[   ] Managing operations
[   ] Other _____

## Part Two: Taking Stock of the Status Quo

It's not uncommon to take the very things that enabled you to grow your business for granted. For instance, you may have come to depend upon critical features of your firm, such as its tech stack or quick access to support from branch management. So, in these next few questions, we ask you to take stock of the status quo, identifying qualities of your current firm that you would want to replicate should you decide to leave, as well as those you might want to improve upon.

3. **What do you like most about your firm?**
   I want you to think deeply here. Be sure to consider things like culture, the community of advisors, your leadership team, the size of the organization, the brand, and everything that serves you well in serving clients and growing your business.

4. **What resources and support do you rely on most (such as platform, technology, back-office capabilities, product support, or firm leadership)?**

5. **What, if anything, frustrates you? What is the impact of each frustration? To what extent do these frustrations limit your ability to reach your goals?**

   Again, I want you to think deeply here. Be rigorously honest about everything that is less than ideal about your current situation, *not* because you are necessarily going to make a move, but because knowledge is power, and I want you to feel empowered by self-awareness. For each item, include how it impacts your work.

6. **Have you tried to remedy any of these issues? What was the result?**

7. **Do you feel you derive enough value from your firm relative to your payout or take-home pay?**

## Part Three: Envisioning Perfection

This section asks that you envision your future and define what you perceive as perfection in terms of your own objectives and the business you're building. It's worth noting that achieving perfection in and of itself is most likely an unrealistic and elusive goal. In reality, perfection doesn't exist anywhere, not even at your current firm. But we ask you to envision what you deem as perfect because it creates a means of comparison between what you have now and what you see as ideal. And, ultimately, the decision of stay versus go will be about determining which version of less-than-perfect is more desirable.

8. **What are your goals: short term, midterm, and long term? Where do you see yourself five and ten years from now? Are you still with your current firm, and at the end of your career would you feel entirely satisfied if you were?**

9. **Do you and your partners share the same goals? If not, how would you reconcile the differences?**

10. **If you could imagine the perfect firm, what would be its top three attributes?**

11. **From a financial perspective, and considering there will be trade-offs, on a scale of 1 to 4 (with 4 being most important), how would you rank these in order of importance?**
    _____ Transition package
    _____ Net payout
    _____ Ownership of your own business
    _____ Equity in a larger entity

## Part Four: Taking a Reality Check on Portability

This is what we call the reality check: taking the pulse of your business as it is today and whether it's ready to make a move should you decide to do so.

12. How confident are you in your depth of client relationships, pipeline, and growth?

13. If you were to make a change, what elements of portability concern you?

## Part Five: Envisioning a More Perfect Future

Putting all else aside, this final question encourages you to be creative and describe your perfect future. What does it look like? What are you doing differently? How has your business changed? How have you changed? And, ultimately...

14. How do you want to live your business life?

## Recap

This exercise was an opportunity for you to assess the status quo with rigorous honesty, examine what's realistic and what's not, and envision the perfect scenario to set as your true north.

We've found that the answers to the questions posed in this self-assessment, combined with an understanding of the options available in the industry landscape, help define a focused and strategic due diligence path, one that empowers you with greater clarity whether you decide to make a move or choose to stay put.

In the next chapter, I'll help you to understand more about what your answers to the questions posed here could mean and to connect the dots between them and your vision and goals so you can assess whether there is congruence with your firm and how you are living your business life.

Ultimately, this will guide you closer to answering the question: *SHOULD I STAY OR SHOULD I GO?*

# Chapter Four

## Connecting the Dots: The Meaning Behind Your Answers

After decades of counseling advisors, it became apparent that there was often one critical step that advisors missed during the due diligence process. That step was taking the time to gain perspective and clarity on their goals—and challenging the notion of whether they could achieve those goals best at their current firm or a new one.

The failure to invest the time to assess their current business life—or even to consider what a potentially better one might look like—led some advisors to stay put by default, others to spin their wheels in a haphazard exploration process, and still others to leave for another firm or model that was ultimately not the right fit.

But those who had clarity around their personal reality— that is, their business life as it was and the business life they desired—as well as what they would have to gain to justify the hassle of a move, got closer to answering the stay-or-go question in the most efficient manner.

Without real clarity around your goals, it's impossible to recognize whether your current firm or a new one will allow you to achieve them.

In this chapter, I discuss what your answers to the questions in the previous chapter might mean, and I help you to connect the dots by identifying where any gaps exist between where you are now and where you really want to be.

There are no right or wrong answers. The idea is to create an honest appraisal of your vision and to ultimately define a strategic blueprint to achieve it.

Keep in mind that the clarity gained in the exercise may reveal that your current firm serves you best—and that's perfectly fine, as the goal of this book is not to sell you on making a move, but rather to help you answer the question of whether to stay or go.

## Part One: Understanding the Impact of *Why* and *What* on Your Decision-Making Process

The two questions in this part asked you to think deeply about what sparks you most about the work that you do.

1.  As Simon Sinek suggests in his bestselling book, *Start With Why*, ask yourself *why* you are a financial advisor. What motivates you?

Question one reflects upon the premise of Simon Sinek's bestselling book *Start With Why*—and it is perhaps the threshold question to ask yourself. The motivation behind *why* you are a financial advisor serves as the foundation upon which what you do and how you do it are built.

Oftentimes, advisors live their lives as if the tail wags the dog. They do things by rote—mechanically moving through each day, checking off one task after another until the day is done. Yet we find that advisors who are clear about their *why* view their work from a different perspective; they are more purposeful and passionate because their actions and goals are rooted in their *raison d'être*.

In considering this question, the most common responses we see relate to client service: helping them solve problems; serving as their financial quarterback; making the complex feel simple; and, most importantly, helping them meet their life goals, to name a few.

---

2. **What aspects of your job as a financial advisor do you find most rewarding? (Check all that apply.)**

   [ ] Managing client relationships
   [ ] Prospecting
   [ ] Financial planning
   [ ] Investment management
   [ ] Managing a team
   [ ] Leading a business
   [ ] Managing operations
   [ ] Other

---

You might expect that the *why* for many advisors centers on their own personal financial security; it would be naive to think otherwise. And that brings us to an important point:

Maximizing the potential for excellence in client service *and* maximizing one's financial well-being don't have to be mutually exclusive. Actually, it's quite the opposite. The ability to provide the best in client service typically drives greater productivity and fulfillment and strengthens the business for the long term. Your personal economics should be an important priority, but not your first.

As Sinek puts it, "Happiness comes from *what* we do. Fulfillment comes from *why* we do it."

When there is congruence between the things you must do and the things you love to do, you will automatically be more energized, productive, and present—and ultimately a better steward for your clients. Unfortunately, some may feel they have to do it all because they don't have support, or their firm is falling short, and they need to pick up the pieces.

> "Happiness comes from *what* we do.
> Fulfillment comes from *why* we do it."
>
> -Simon Sinek

So, in question two, we take a deeper look at what you do on a daily basis to glean what's most soulful and to identify those tasks that you might consider off-loading to others who are better suited to handle them.

It's an important dialogue to have with yourself because the reality is that while you may be capable of doing many things, "doing it all" does not make for a fulfilling path to success. So, take the time to assess what you are doing now and then consider what that list would look like in an ideal world.

Gaining clarity on what you like to do best and what your core competencies are versus what you should outsource or off-load is a critical step in the self-exploration process, regardless of whether you're looking to make a change or not.

## Part Two: Taking Stock of the Status Quo

With this group of questions, I ask that you take a close look at your business and assess everything you rely upon to make it run—even the things you take most for granted, including operations, compliance, legal, branch management, and tech support. The point is to examine those things that would be most critical to replicate if you were to make a move.

3. What do you like most about your firm?
4. What resources and support do you rely on most (such as platform, technology, back-office capabilities, product support, or firm leadership)?

It's important not to overlook features you might miss if they were gone, such as the ability to pick up the phone and have tech support at your desk in minutes, a branch manager available to block and tackle, the camaraderie of working with like-minded colleagues, the office with its fully stocked refrigerator, and the parking deck that offers quick access to your corner office with the fabulous view.

It's equally vital to identify where you feel limited or stuck. Even if you are committed to staying put, awareness of the issues will drive you to more proactively find solutions.

We believe in the philosophy of "do no harm." As an advisor, you never want to do less for clients than what you're currently doing for them. Being clear on what resources are important helps to narrow the options. For example, if access to a big firm's balance sheet, brand, and syndicate offerings is critical to the service of your ultra-high-net-worth clients, that fact will help you eliminate many of the options that are not major financial institutions. Or, if you have entrepreneurial DNA that is not being tapped now, perhaps you might explore options that would give you more freedom, flexibility, and control.

For some advisors, this exercise of putting pen to paper enables them to realize that they are well-served at their firm, while it may reveal previously unexamined gaps for others.

> **5.** **What, if anything, frustrates you? What is the impact of each frustration? To what extent do these frustrations limit your ability to reach your goals?**

While every question in the self-assessment is important in its own right, number five is one of the most powerful.

It's here that I ask you to focus on the negatives, not to create drama where none exists, but rather to encourage you to be rigorously self-aware and brutally honest about the realities of your professional life.

This is a critical point: *In any situation, awareness and acknowledgement of the truth leads to empowerment—that is, the power to choose how you will respond.*

Make no mistake: It takes courage to be willing to get real about life's imperfections. Because the path of least resistance would be to blissfully ignore what's not quite right and accept the status quo.

> Only you can determine if the status quo serves you well enough.

But not all things that frustrate you are necessarily equal. Some are no more than minor annoyances that can, and should, be easy to overlook or work through. Others, whether individually or in combination, might be more intolerable and motivate you toward change.

Perhaps the best illustration of this is by personal example. My husband, Howard, is a wonderful man and the greatest supporter of all things that I do. But he has a couple of habits that drive me crazy: He regularly leaves the cap off the toothpaste tube and dirty dishes in the sink. Are these minor annoyances? Absolutely. Are they divorce-worthy? Definitely not, because despite these behaviors, Howard is otherwise the very best husband I could ever imagine.

Another example more relevant to the industry might be that a firm doesn't allow for communicating with clients via text message. Is this a minor annoyance, or does it hamper your productivity and your ability to serve clients optimally? Some advisors would say, "This policy makes my life untenable, and I can't live with it." Others might say, "I wish it were different, but this one particular policy does not materially affect my business life."

So, this is where you should make the key distinction: If the sum total of the things that frustrate you add up to no more than some minor annoyances, then it is likely good enough to stay put. But, typically, the advisors who choose to change firms acknowledge glaring frustrations—irritants well beyond dishes left in the sink—that are very much limiting their ability to serve clients and grow their businesses. Ultimately, frustrations alone should never be the sole driving force behind changing firms or models. That is a choice that you need to equally root in the pull *toward* something better, as I will address shortly.

Nothing in life is perfect. Every advisor's tolerance for those imperfections is different. This is a personal exercise; only you can determine if your firm serves you well enough.

> 6. **Have you tried to remedy any of these issues? What was the result?**

Before making any major decisions about your professional life, it's important to know that you've done everything you can to improve your situation, because the path of least resistance is always to stay put. And without giving it your all, you may always wonder what could have been. This may include speaking to your local branch manager or even escalating your concerns to those in more senior leadership positions.

> 7. **Do you feel you derive enough value from your firm relative to your payout or take-home pay?**

Brokerage firms charge a hefty tariff for operating on their platform. For employee advisors, giving up more than fifty cents on every dollar of revenue may feel annoying, especially considering how the true net take-home becomes significantly less when factoring in out-of-pocket expenses like support staff bonuses, as well as incremental travel and client entertainment costs. Even so, unequivocally, there is value to the service your firm provides. With that in mind, question seven asks you if you're getting your money's worth: Are the platform, technology, human capital, and operational support robust enough to justify the amount you pay to use them?

During the COVID-19 pandemic, this question was especially top-of-mind for advisors across the industry. Working remotely and being more self-sufficient was a major shift that led many to realize that they no longer relied upon their firms' resources as much as they did in the past. As a result, many opted to move to firms or models offering greater independence.

Ultimately, the goal of this section is to better understand, on par, how well your firm is serving you and if there are any conflicts or limitations preventing you from delivering optimal service to your clients.

## Part Three: Envisioning Perfection

In the previous chapter, I cautioned that perfection can be an elusive goal. Yet knowing what you perceive as perfect serves as a guide for comparison between your current firm and another, and, ultimately, the basis for determining which version of less-than-perfect works better for you.

> Knowing what you perceive as
> perfect serves as a guide for
> comparison between your current
> firm and another.

In this section, I ask that you take a bigger-picture look at your true north: the vision and principles that serve as the foundation upon which you are building your business. And that means thinking deeply to honestly define your goals, both for the long term and short term, and about what might constitute a more perfect scenario.

But often, advisors are afraid to picture what their ideal business and future look like, because that may indicate that change will be required to achieve it. And this is where many get stuck in inertia and instead opt to accept their current situation, whether it serves them best or not.

It's easy to kick the proverbial can down the road when it comes to thinking about change, especially at a time when business is growing and market conditions are favorable. It's hard to make time to work *on* the business instead of *in* it.

8. **What are your goals: short term, midterm, and long term? Where do you see yourself five and ten years from now? Are you still with your current firm, and at the end of your career would you feel entirely satisfied if you were?**

But when we courageously ask ourselves "Am I living my best business life?", the metaphor of the trapeze we discussed in chapter one comes to mind, because it highlights the gap between where you are and where you want to be. The future goals of the business are the next trapeze bar—and the longer you wait, the harder it will be to reach.

The reality is that complacency is the enemy of all great businesses. Consider the case of Blockbuster Video, which failed to jump on the digital bandwagon as customer expectations, viewing habits, and access were changing around it, leaving the door open for Netflix to fill the gap. By the time Blockbuster woke up, it was too late. It's a cautionary story for all business owners, and advisors are no exception. Those who focus solely on the short term and ignore signs of change around them run the risk of limiting their potential, options, and profitability in the long run.

## Complacency is the enemy of all great businesses.

When thinking through both your short- and long-term goals, it's important to imagine yourself five or ten years down the road, paying close attention to what you'd like your business life to look like. Yet, having that vision isn't possible if you limit your horizons.

Over the years, the savviest advisors we worked with stayed regularly educated on the world beyond their immediate four walls—even if they weren't entertaining the thought of making a change. They worked with coaches to clarify their goals and vision, and they exchanged ideas with peers at other firms, ensuring they were always challenging their thinking and holding themselves to the highest standards.

It's also worth noting that what's changed the most in the past decade is advisor mindset, shifting from a focus on the short term to thinking about the bigger picture. As advisors think of their business as an enterprise instead of a practice, the question of how they can best maximize its value moves front and center, whether achieving that value is ultimately via their firm's retire-in-place program or in a transition.

With this background knowledge, you can then ask yourself, "In a perfect world, would I be disappointed if I'm still with my current firm?"

> 9. Do you and your partners share the same goals? If not, how would you reconcile the differences?

In the past decade, senior leaders at brokerage firms have worked hard to encourage, and in some cases, mandate, advisors to form ensemble practices.

Team structures are better for the firm because multiple stakeholders with disparate risk tolerances make it less likely that all parties share the same sentiments when it comes to envisioning the future.

In any case, a team construct can be better for clients because they get more well-rounded service and expertise from a team. And this setup can be better for advisors when partnerships are rooted in trust, shared vision, and goals.

Unfortunately, many partnerships, even those once formed for the right reasons, can grow apart over time.

Nothing can highlight the differences between partners more than thinking about the future of the business and about whether a change of firm or model is warranted. Achieving clarity on partnership functions—and whether all partners have equal voices—is a critical first step. Are decisions made as a democracy or is there a senior partner whose opinions supersede all others?

It's also important to know where each key stakeholder stands in terms of their goals for themselves and the business and to identify how much daylight there is between those goals and reality. Only then can you assess the gap that may exist between you and your partner or partners.

It's at this stage where there can be significant pressure on the relationship, because even if all parties agree about what's imperfect, not everyone may have the same risk appetite to do something about it. As an illustration, think about a scenario where everyone agrees that change is needed, but one partner prefers the familiarity and convenience of an all-under-one-roof big firm, while others may want to swing for the fences and go fully independent.

Going into any due diligence process with your eyes wide open will allow you to devise a plan on how best to move forward. Identifying irreconcilable differences before you begin exploration will prevent you from spinning your wheels during the due diligence process.

The topic of partnerships is an important one that I take a closer look at in chapter seven.

> **10.** **If you could imagine the perfect firm, what would be its top three attributes?**

This question assumes you're strongly considering a move. And the truth of the matter is the answer is one that many advisors struggle with because it can be difficult to take a step back from your current situation and imagine what perfection really looks like when you've been wearing the same firm's goggles for so long.

## Take a moment to think big and without limitation.

So, take a moment to think big and without limitation. By analogy, when deciding where to vacation, you may limit yourself to only the places you're familiar with or destinations within a certain radius. But I'm asking you to rid yourself of the "knowns," clear your mind, and dream *big*. Imagine going to parts of the world that could be more exciting, albeit culturally unfamiliar. Then consider the types of activities you'd like to do while on vacation, such as exploring ancient ruins, diving deep-sea wrecks, or simply finding a secluded beach to relax on. Taking this type of perspective will offer you the chance to think not just about where you want to go, but also what you'd like to do once you get there.

Even if you're pretty sure you have no intention of making a change, give yourself permission to picture perfection. This exercise can allow you to create something better, even within your current firm, because many don't recognize perfection until they've taken the time to deeply consider how it aligns with their goals.

You might find this question easier to answer by taking stock of your business as it currently stands and evaluating it client-by-client. Then ask yourself:

- Are each client's needs being fully met?
- If not, what's missing?
- Even if my clients don't know they are missing something, what services would I like to be able to offer them?
- What would it take to meet their needs?
- What's blocking me from growing the business even faster?
- When I lost a client or prospect opportunity, what was the reason?

Ultimately, this discovery process is about knowing those attributes that are most important to you and your business, assessing the delta between where you are and that vision of perfection, and deciding what you're prepared to do about it, if anything.

---

**11.** **From a financial perspective, and considering there will be trade-offs, on a scale of 1 to 4 (with 4 being most important), how would you rank these in order of importance?**

\_\_\_\_\_ Transition package

\_\_\_\_\_ Net payout

\_\_\_\_\_ Ownership of your own business

\_\_\_\_\_ Equity in a larger entity

---

While you considered the attributes of a perfect firm in the previous question, this question shifts the focus to the economics. Just as in the previous question, understanding what's most important will enable you to direct your efforts toward the right firms or models, and you'll come to the table with an understanding of how you expect to get closest to your ideal scenario.

Any firm's transition package may include multiple components to incentivize recruitment. That's why it's critical to know what might be part of an offer, such as up-front cash, back-end earnouts, accelerated payout (or net payout), equity, and book ownership, and to evaluate the importance of each before getting to the negotiation phase.

With some firms, there is little to no wiggle room in how they structure deals. But others will customize a transition package based on the advisor prospect's needs. For example, with the wirehouses, deals are largely formulaic (based on a structure that dictates the amounts at various production levels) and not up for negotiation. And depending upon how much revenue a recruit generates, there will be a set amount for cash offered, unvested deferred compensation that will be reimbursed, and back-end growth incentives to be included.

Models outside of the wirehouse world are quite different. Regional, boutique, and independent firms may be more willing to customize the deals they write based on what's important to the recruit. With an independent firm and some boutique firms, for example, if an advisor wants to participate in the growth of the overall enterprise, then equity can be a very compelling form of currency.

Yet other advisors may value the greatest amount of cash in a deal, with a focus on the short-term upside and removing risk from the move. However, firms that offer the most up-front cash are typically doing so at the expense of an advisor creating long-term enterprise value, since the advisor is likely joining as a captive employee, often with lower payouts than their independent counterparts.

On the other hand, many advisors take a longer-term view, prioritizing the ability to build enterprise value and ultimately monetize the business for the greatest possible multiple. For example, advisors who opt to build their own RIA firm do so without the security of a large up-front transition deal, but they receive a significantly higher net payout and will ultimately own a business that they can monetize down the line with long-term capital gains tax treatment.

Without the knowledge of your own expectations and the ability to align those with the realities of the marketplace, exploring will send you down the proverbial rabbit hole: a due diligence process that feels more frustrating than fruitful.

> Without the knowledge of your expectations and the ability to align those with the realities of the marketplace, due diligence can become more frustrating than fruitful.

## Part Four: Taking a Reality Check on Portability

This section addresses the questions that often keep those thinking of changing firms up at night. And for good reason: After investing a professional lifetime around building and nurturing relationships, the last thing an advisor wants to do is lose ground.

The topic of client portability is a very common concern. Sometimes it can be rooted in the reality that the advisor has not developed strong enough relationships based on mutual trust. But, even for those who have strong relationships, there are always unforeseen factors that can influence portability. An advisor considering change must be comfortable accepting a certain amount of risk and be rigorously self-aware about the depth of their relationships.

However, our experience has been that 85 percent to 95 percent of the clients the advisor wanted to take with them followed within six months. This is typically true for advisors who have always put client interests first and who can clearly demonstrate that their move is being made for their clients' benefit. The ultimate litmus test to determine whether there is enough value in a move for your clients is to ask yourself, "What's in it for them?"

> **12.** **How confident are you in your depth of client relationships, pipeline, and growth?**

First and foremost, you must assess your relationships one by one to determine the legitimacy of portability concerns. That means understanding the depth and nature of your relationships and your ability to serve and nurture them at a new firm or model. We counsel every advisor to take the pulse of their relationships periodically so that they know where they stand at all times, even if they aren't considering a move.

The good news is that it has become far more typical for clients to develop long-standing connections with their advisors, not the firm they represent. However, even in the best of circumstances, if a firm or model you are considering can't meet a client's needs, then that would likely put portability of that client in jeopardy.

To fully understand which clients may not benefit from or even be hurt by your move requires a more in-depth analysis of your book to review all holdings—including asset managers, alternative investments, securities-backed loans, and platform pricing—to determine any non-portable positions. You must be cognizant of the result that leaving those positions or clients behind would have on your overall business.

This question is not intended to replace a book mapping exercise (in which the firm you're considering vets every position in your book to see how each will port over) that allows for a deeper dive and comes later in the due diligence process. The goal is to simply create awareness of your client relationships and the ability to serve them best.

Once you have a clear picture of your client relationships, consider your prospects for the future. Take the time to assess whether your current firm supports your vision for growth, or if a change in firms or models will allow you to increase your potential. For example, if you are thinking about bringing the business more upmarket, what do you believe higher-net-worth prospects are ideally attracted to? And do those attributes exist at your current firm?

For more on the topic of assessing client relationships and portability, see chapter seven.

Often the concern over portability arises from an unrealistic view of one's client relationships. Taking an honest appraisal of those relationships allows you to approach change with clear expectations of the outcome.

> **13.** **If you were to make a change, what elements of portability concern you?**

Still, plenty of advisors are held captive by the worry that their clients are committed to the brand of their current firm. While this could be true in some cases, in most, advisors sell themselves short when they allow fear to rule them, especially when the potential upside of a new opportunity could outweigh any loss. Today, loyalty is much more about a client's relationship with their individual advisor and their advisor's ability to serve them, which makes clients more willing to follow their advisor to a new firm or model than they might have been in the past.

Bear in mind that it's rare for 100 percent of clients to follow their advisor to a new firm, so you need to be clear about what your level of acceptable loss is. That raises the notion of what we call "shrink to grow": a strategic choice to leave a portion of assets behind because you believe the business would be better served overall and grow faster in an environment that is better aligned with your vision and goals.

> Maximizing portability is about the strength of client relationships and the advisor's ability to serve them best.

Ultimately, maximizing portability is about the strength of client relationships and the advisor's ability to serve them best. So, use the time before considering a move to ensure you've properly solidified relationships, and you'll find that the right clients will follow—along with the success you seek.

## Part Five: Envisioning a More Perfect Future

> **14.** **How do you want to live your business life?**

Throughout this exercise, you've stepped back to take a hard look at what you are doing now and what you want to be doing—with an ultimate goal of identifying the delta between the two and assessing the changes you're willing to make to bridge the gap.

So, this final question encourages you to be creative and envision your perfect future to determine what you would find most soulful.

By "soulful" I mean:

- Being better connected to yourself and doing what feels right and makes you feel fulfilled.
- Living in a way that better aligns with your values and doesn't leave you divided.
- Being present and able to give all of yourself to your work because you are sparked and excited.

And it means considering with complete honesty and candor the answers to questions like:

- What would my best business life look like?
- What would I be doing differently?
- How would my business have to change?
- How would I have to change?
- How have my clients' needs changed over time?
- Who would carry on my legacy?
- How would I get from here to there?
- What changes am I willing to make to do so?

## Recap

Up to this point, I hope you've gained insights into your personal reality. Your head may be spinning with new thoughts and ideas. And that's a perfect result.

Ultimately, the value of this exercise is knowledge—and knowledge is power. Establishing what's most important to your life's work—including the value you place on control, flexibility, and ownership—is what will help you to eliminate inertia and open your mind to new possibilities.

So even if you choose to stay put, the insights you gleaned in this exercise will enable you to do so from a position of greater strength, and with an invigorated sense of determination and commitment.

But for those of you not sold on staying, you may recognize an uncomfortable gap between where you are now and where you want to be, edging you closer to answering the fundamental question, "Should I stay or should I go?"

With your newfound knowledge and a good dose of open-mindedness, let's take a deeper dive into answering that challenge.

# Chapter Five

# Due Diligence: What You Don't Know Could Surprise You

Perhaps you have now identified a gap between where you are and where you want to be. You should have clarity around the answers to these four questions regarding that gap:

- How unhappy am I, and am I willing to do something about it?
- How important is transition money?
- How flexible am I willing to be to reach my goals?
- What's most important to my clients?

Essentially, it's that gap that helps determine the urgency around the next steps you might take. If the gap is big enough and important enough to justify the hassle of a move, then it makes sense to begin due diligence. You may decide that a more passive approach, which I call "armchair exploration," is enough to educate you about the possibilities that exist beyond your firm. Or you may feel greater urgency and opt for a more active form of due diligence: taking meetings with representatives of other firms and engaging in a true compare and contrast of all possible options.

Either way, taking the time to get educated is a smart business decision, regardless of whether you want or are ready to make a move. Being a student of the industry—knowing how it is changing and becoming aware of the growing list of options available—will no doubt empower you to become a better advisor and, even more so, a fiduciary to your clients. This understanding will allow you to know, with certainty, that you are delivering the very best of what's available to your clients.

> Full awareness of your goals, plus basic knowledge of the industry landscape, will allow you to weigh options against the status quo.

Yet many advisors shy away from the due diligence process itself, envisioning an exhaustive barrage of calls from recruiters and managers at other firms and meetings that often lead nowhere. But it doesn't have to be that way. Having full awareness of your goals, plus basic knowledge of the industry landscape, will allow you to weigh options against the status quo in the most productive and efficient manner, with your current firm serving as the benchmark with which to compare every other option.

## Best Practices to Consider

For those who have decided to embark upon an active due diligence process, whether with a recruiter or on your own, there are ways to make it both strategic and efficient. Barbara Herman, senior vice president and top recruiter from our team, wrote an article[5] that shares ten tips to help steer you in the right direction:

1. **Arm yourself with a solid understanding of the landscape and insights from your self-assessment.**
   Based on this information, what options will you consider and what is the time line? Revisit this list of options frequently and modify as appropriate.

2. **View everything from your clients' perspective.**
   What's in it for them? Think about the message you would deliver to clients should you opt to make a move, citing the benefits they would see. Is "what's in it for them" enough to justify any disruption they may experience?

3. **Don't allow yourself to be blinded by the big check.**
   Certainly, being compensated for the hassle of making a move is an important consideration. Most advisors wouldn't—or shouldn't—go elsewhere without being certain that the financials of the transition were appropriate. While understanding the economics of a recruiting package is important, it shouldn't be your first inquiry. It sends the wrong message about your intent to another

---

5   Barbara Herman, "Surviving Due Diligence: 10 Tips for Financial Advisors," January 2020, https://www.diamond-consultants.com/guide-surviving-due-diligence-process/.

firm. Ultimately, the real driving factor for a move should be centered around your clients and not the deal. (I will explore this topic more in depth in the next chapter.)

4. **Be sure you're not running from your frustrations, but toward your goals.**
Every move should be driven by a series of pushes and pulls. The pushes are pain points or frustrations that an advisor is looking to solve for, leave behind, and run from. The pulls are what advisors are most excited about: the real potential that a new opportunity represents. Moving motivated by pushes alone can be a mistake. There needs to be an equal or greater number of pulls drawing you somewhere else to balance the risk and hassle that comes with a move.

5. **Take a 10,000-foot view of your business.**
Put some thought into which clients will follow you and those you might prefer to leave behind. Assess what you will need to replicate and identify which clients may be hard to move or require special consideration, as I discussed in the previous chapter. And be clear about the amount of loss you'd be willing to tolerate.

6. **If you are in a partnership, be sure everyone is on board with the plan.**
Identify each partner's specific goals and determine if you are aligned as a team. Be clear on how you will make decisions and what happens if there isn't a consensus. (I will have more to say about this in chapter seven.)

7. **Get—and stay—organized.**
   Develop a process for keeping track of open items, questions, and who is responsible for follow-up. (Later in this chapter, I offer a framework that you can use to help guide your process.)

8. **Keep your circle close. Limit who knows of your plans to only those who need to know.**
   Avoid openly discussing your thoughts and actions outside this circle and only widen it to include key team members when it is essential to do so. The words "discretion" and "confidentiality" are critical so that you can make any move on your time line and not in fire-drill mode because you've been found out.

9. **Maintain the status quo.**
   Don't alter your behavior such as suddenly printing reports or taking conspicuous absences from the office. Avoid any actions or attitudes that are uncharacteristic, and always be a good corporate citizen. Don't give anyone at your firm reason to believe you might be a flight risk.

10. **Speak with an attorney.**
    Obtaining the advice of legal counsel is a vital step to understanding and remaining in compliance with Protocol (where applicable), any and all post-employment restrictions, and new regulatory requirements. Review your compliance history, as this can impact and possibly complicate a move. I'm asked a lot if it is essential for an advisor considering change to hire their own counsel even

though most any firm you would join will have its legal team guide the transition process. I believe it is critical for any advisor who is changing firms to retain an attorney who would represent their interests alone. In most cases, it's appropriate to wait to bring this attorney on board until you have decided *that* you are going, *where* you are going, and *when*.

> In situations where it's a close call between a new opportunity or your current firm, the tie goes to your current firm.

And, most importantly, keep your current firm at the top of the list of possible choices. You must compare every option you evaluate with what you already have. A new opportunity needs to be better than your firm and more than better enough overall. But in situations where it's a close call between a new opportunity or your current firm, we believe that the tie should go to your current firm.

## But What is Better Enough?

There might be certain aspects of another firm or model that appeal to you, but when you consider the whole, if it isn't more than marginally better than where you are now, then it's likely not better enough to justify the risk and hassle of a move.

The concept of "better enough" relates to two key areas:

- The ability to serve clients better.
- The ability to grow faster.

That brings us to another important point: There is no perfection, whether at your current firm or any other. Yet there are still many advisors who get stuck trying to check every box on their wish list. The more motivated you are to move, the more flexible you will need to be—while always prioritizing what's most important to you.

> ## A new opportunity that is only marginally better isn't better enough.

Keep in mind that the goal of a due diligence process should be to find clarity that will allow you to make an informed decision, even if you wind up staying right where you are. Ultimately, you'll come away with, at the very least, an enhanced understanding of the evolved industry landscape. While you may have embarked upon due diligence thinking that a move was in order, the end result may be that you choose to stay put because you haven't found an option that would be better enough. In that case, the bonus is that you can carry on with a renewed commitment to your firm from a position of greater strength.

## Be Willing to Take Those Meetings

There is no substitute for taking meetings with other firms or evaluating other models, because you will learn things that you can't any other way. Sure, a good recruiter or even a colleague who works at a firm you are considering can paint a picture of what life might look like. However, the best way to learn how a new firm would meet your specific needs, and to get a first-hand sense of culture and ethos, is to meet the firm's most relevant leaders. Plus, the process opens your eyes to new possibilities, ensuring that your thinking doesn't become insular—it has the added benefit of keeping you on the radar of the competition. Being strategic about which meetings to take is critical. The knowledge gained in the self-assessment process I described earlier in this book should help guide that decision.

> The more strategic and thoughtful you are, the fewer meetings you will need to take and the greater the likelihood of a positive investment of your time.

Determine how you would like to conduct the first meeting (by phone, on a videoconferencing platform like Zoom, or face to face) and if someone on your team should be there with you—while, of course, *maintaining strict confidentiality*. This is when you need to balance the benefit of empowering the team while keeping the circle tight: including only those you can trust and who are essential. (If you are working with an attorney who understands advisor transitions, obtaining guidance around who to involve in the due diligence process and when to do so is appropriate.)

Some teams believe conducting due diligence is a joint effort resulting in one of the most important decisions they will make. As such, they have every partner attend every meeting, so that all stay informed and current. Others elect one point person to have the initial round of meetings, so as not to take every partner out of business at the same time.

Strategic due diligence is all about taking the right meetings and part of that is not oversaturating your search with too many options. Put another way, the more strategic and thoughtful you are in curating your alternatives, the fewer meetings you will need to take—and the greater the likelihood each will result in a positive investment of your time. Typically, we recommend that advisors conduct due diligence on no more than four firms at once, as it's better to go deeper with a select group of firms than to go too wide and risk staying at the surface level during the discovery process.

There is no right or wrong approach here. Whichever way you choose to attack due diligence, remember that both you and the firm you investigate will be looking at suitability and fit. The people you meet will be evaluating you as much as you will be appraising them. They will want to see how you interact with your teammates and partners. And they will pay attention to how much respect you convey to those with whom you are meeting. Many successful advisors go into these situations believing that they hold all the cards because their book of business is impressive in size, but they forget that the evaluation process goes both ways. Firms measure the cultural match just as much as you do. And, ultimately, hiring managers and firm recruiters fight for advisors they like, which may lead to a better economic package.

## A True Compare-and-Contrast Process

To conduct deep and thorough due diligence and to really get to know a firm, you'll likely have two to three meetings with the local or regional manager and, in many instances, senior leadership. This is an opportunity for you to get acquainted with them and assess whether they are a team you would want to work for. If you're interested in going further, then you will have phone conversations or face-to-face meetings with heads of product areas relevant to your business (such as banking, insurance, trust and estates, and alternative investments).

Technology and platform demonstrations are critical next steps in the process, as is talking with advisors who have joined the firm. Diving deeper yet typically means a home office visit, where you take the better part of a day to meet key people in the organization who may have an impact on your transition and business in the long run.

> The home office visit is a critical opportunity to assess a new firm's ethos and culture.

The home office visit is a critical opportunity to assess a new firm's ethos and culture. While culture is one of the most overused words in the financial services industry—every firm touts its "outstanding culture"—the truth is that not all cultures are created equal. So, it's important to get a sense of what a firm stands for and how it supports its advisors and their clients and to assess whether its beliefs and principles are congruent with yours.

The visit gives you an opportunity to develop personal relationships with key support resources and is an efficient way to round out the due diligence process. Ultimately, it's when you get to demonstrate your unique value and interest level, which gives you leverage in negotiating an optimal recruitment deal.

In most cases, advisors who want to explore their options will look at multiple firms. But it is far too exhausting and time consuming to get fully immersed in more than one or two. Somewhere along the way, you will need to cull the opportunity set—the options that most closely align with your goals—to your top choices.

While it's most important for you to conduct due diligence on a firm, it will also conduct due diligence on you. This means that you will need to provide official production and asset reports, authorize a check of your CRD (FINRA's Central Registration Depository of registration records), allow credit checks, and complete firm-specific documents. At this stage, it's also vital to be proactive and disclose any potential or ongoing compliance issues.

We are asked a lot about the risk of going too deep with a firm during the recruiting process. For example: If you provide all the documentation required and have your CRD pulled, will it raise a red flag with your current firm? The answer is "no." As long as you are exploring quality firms and meeting representatives you have faith in and respect for, you can trust that your information is being held in strict confidence. Advisors who get found out are almost always those who share their plans beyond their circle of trust, color outside the lines, or otherwise "poke the bear."

## The Seven Key Areas for Evaluation

To help keep things organized, we created a Due Diligence Playbook (available on the resources page at https://www. diamond-consultants.com/book-resources/), which serves as a framework for the exploration process. It provides a structure by which our advisor-clients can efficiently gather the most relevant information to differentiate between firms and zero in on the one or two that can best support their business and serve their clients.

There are seven key areas for evaluation:

- Culture.
- Freedom and control.
- Support for growth.
- Technology.
- Platform.
- Economics.
- Specialized services.

Below is a synopsis of each of these focus areas and a sampling of some of the specifics that you will gather during the due diligence process for use as the basis for comparing and contrasting options. We strongly encourage that you also assess your current firm using the same criteria.

### Culture

The intrinsic value of organizational culture has gained traction over recent years, particularly in the wealth management world. This is especially true now that nearly everything that an advisor needs to access is largely commoditized. It seems that every firm says their culture is "better than all others." Given that not all cultures are created equal, it is critical to determine if the firm's shared system of beliefs and vision aligns with your own.

Culture can be difficult to appraise as an outsider, so we suggest asking the following basic questions:

- What is your advisor attrition rate?
- When you lose advisors, what are the main reasons they opt to leave?
- And, most importantly, what are the firm's beliefs about who owns the clients?

**Freedom and Control**

The ongoing battle for control between firms and advisors has created one of the most common drivers of movement away from the wirehouse world and toward models (such as regional and boutique firms) that offer advisors the chance to gain greater agency over their professional lives. The overall ability to run your business as you see fit, including complete control over the investment process, client service model, take-home compensation, and marketing and branding happens in the independent space.

To gain a full understanding of the level of freedom and control you can expect, consider asking the following questions:

- Can I use outside platforms or am I captive to just one?

- Will I be able to self-brand and create a website that is unique to my business? How will I be able to market myself?
- How often does this firm change advisor compensation?
- What's the process or likelihood of being granted exceptions?

You should also provide examples of client needs you have been unable to meet and expect suggestions from a new firm on how those needs might be fulfilled if you were to join.

## Support for Growth

Ultimately, the goal of any advisor is to grow their business, so understanding the role that a new firm or model plays in facilitating growth is vital. At the end of the day, while each advisor is responsible for their own growth, a firm will either be an accelerant or an impediment. Questions like the following can help you determine which of these categories the firm belongs to:

- Will I have the freedom to hire new team members as I see fit?
- Will I have the ability to leverage subject matter experts and senior leadership for important new business opportunities?
- Is there a referral mechanism for new business?
- What is the firm's policy around compensating third-party centers of influence (those who have the ability to refer business to you)?

- Can you give me examples of how advisors you've recruited in the past five years have grown?
- How do you expect that joining your firm will further accelerate my growth?

This is a very important question, which should garner a very telling answer. Every manager tasked with recruiting says that they will help accelerate an advisor's growth should they join—but *by what means* they will do so is most meaningful. So, listen for specificity.

## Technology

Access to modern technology that can make an advisor's practice more efficient and improve their connection with clients should be of utmost importance. Ultimately, you are trying to determine the priority that an organization places on technology, so ask questions like these:

- How sophisticated or customizable are your performance-reporting capabilities?
- Will I be able to report on assets held away, that is, assets not custodied in house?
- How do you believe your firm's technology compares with the Street?
- What technology upgrades are you currently prioritizing?
- In the past few years, how much has the firm invested in technology?
- Does the firm offer integrations with third-party technology platforms, or is the tech stack proprietary?

## Platform

We use the term "platform" to describe access to anything and everything in an advisor's client service toolbox, such as research, investment capabilities, lending, and insurance. So, you might ask:

- What is the firm's approach to banking and lending?
- To what extent can I leverage centrally managed portfolios?
- Will I have open architecture access to the Street with respect to research, alternative investments, and structured products or will I be limited to what the firm offers?
- How does my current roster of managers and strategies map over to the new platform? How do the costs compare?

## Economics

Although a transition is about much more than the dollars and cents, understanding the financial ramifications of a move is essential. So, questions like these should be on your mind:

- What is the firm's compensation plan (or grid) and history for altering compensation over the past few years?
- What percentage of total compensation would be deferred?
- If you were to offer me a transition deal, how would it be structured (up front, back-end growth earnouts, length of note, etc.)?

- Do you reimburse unvested deferred compensation?
- What sort of expense budget and allowance for support staff salaries do you offer?
- Will the firm offer raises to my support staff?

## Specialized Services

In a world where investment advice has become commoditized, clients are looking to their advisors to offer much more than simple portfolio management. With that in mind, understanding how a new firm can help to bolster an advisor's value proposition is important. Additionally, offering value-add services that you can't access at your current firm goes to answer the important question of "What's in it for the clients?" in a move.

Consider asking the following:

- Are there resources to turn to for advanced planning, estate planning, or tax issues that arise?
- For higher-net-worth clients, is there a family office division that may offer bill pay and concierge services?
- Is there access to private investments?
- Does the firm offer support for philanthropy and family governance consulting?

The due diligence process takes time—and can be overwhelming. To help you stay organized, we created a Due Diligence Scorecard (available on the resources page at https://www.diamond-consultants.com/book-resources/).

## Recap

The due diligence process is the ultimate exercise in compare and contrast because you are using your current reality as the benchmark upon which you will evaluate every other option. Yet, some advisors view it as a cumbersome and drawn-out activity that can lead to confusion and overwhelm. Those advisors may not be wrong if they aren't conducting a strategic and thoughtful process.

While every advisor has their own due diligence process and preferences, this chapter offers a best practices approach based upon our experience in guiding our advisor-clients.

Whether you take a more passive approach (armchair exploration) or opt for a more active form involving meetings with representatives of other firms, having a strategy and ultimately curating the list to one or two firms will make the process more efficient and effective.

Keep in mind that the goal of due diligence is to provide you with an enhanced understanding of the evolved industry landscape. The end result may be that you choose to stay put because there isn't an option that you believe to be better enough. Regardless, the knowledge you will have gained is empowering—and demonstrates that you are acting as a fiduciary to your clients, confirming with certainty that you are truly serving them best right where you are.

And when armed with knowledge about your goals and the industry landscape, you can define a path that will lead you toward your best business life.

# Chapter Six

# The Economics and the Negotiation Process

U p to this point, we've looked at the different options available in a greatly expanded industry landscape. Next, we walked through a process to help you identify your goals and use them to pinpoint the options that work best for you from the waterfall of possibilities. What's left is exploring the financial considerations relative to a move.

While money is important, I emphasize again, your personal economics should not be the primary focus—even when monetizing the business you've built is a meaningful priority. It is far more important to make your decision based on what's best for your clients—and your business overall.

That said, no advisor should consider a move without understanding how the economics would be structured to ensure there is enough incentive to justify the hassle and risks of disrupting your professional life. The key is to never get so caught up in the numbers that you lose sight of what you are hoping to achieve.

It's not enough just to understand the numbers, you must also consider whether you're interested in monetizing the business in the short term or if you have the desire to maximize long-term value. And that's critical because it is often a determinant of the options you might consider.

For example, a team of advisors more interested in the long term may ignore the enticement of a sizable cash transition package today (where at least half of the incentive is paid up front), to bet it all on themselves and the ability to build equity and enterprise value as independent business owners. Of course, this team of advisors is still cognizant of the financials and the opportunity cost of eschewing what could be a very significant "bird in the hand," but it places much greater value on the ability to eventually sell its business with long-term capital gains tax treatment for a far higher purchase price. Alternatively, an advisor with no interest in independence or whose focus is shorter term might have more interest in monetizing their business at the time of transition by accepting an aggressive cash recruitment package.

> The key is to never get so caught up in the numbers that you lose sight of what you are hoping to achieve.

Once you have reconciled where you stand on the value of short-term versus long-term economics, we suggest putting a pin in thinking about the transition deal until much later in the process. Why? Because it's more important that an advisor fall in love with a firm or model itself and not be blinded by the numbers.

And, truth be told, most firms are not willing to discuss the transition economics they offer until they have a clear understanding of what an advisor's business looks like, whether they are a good fit, and how motivated the advisor is to join them.

But having reached this chapter, I can assume you're at a point where it's time to address the question: "In terms of transition deals and ongoing economics, what can I expect?"

In the end, the model or firm you choose will determine how a deal is structured and the size of a package, as well as your take-home pay because there is no one-size-fits-all approach.

## Transition Deals in the Wirehouse World

While we use the term "wirehouse" here, it's important to note that we are also referring to other traditional models, such as regional and boutique firms.

As of this writing, deals are at an all-time high. I've said it so often it feels like a platitude. But as competition for advisor talent intensifies, it is truer now more than ever before. Our industry has long confronted an imbalance between supply and demand in which every firm, large and small, seeks to make competitive advisor recruiting a core part of its strategy. Even so, there are not enough productive advisors seeking change to satisfy this appetite. As a result, the most powerful tool a firm has is the recruiting deal.

The most powerful tool a firm has is the recruiting deal.

There's no way to predict where deals go from here, but many firms are already customizing deal structures to better match an advisor's preferences, because the race for top talent has never been more competitive. Firms that want to recruit successfully recognize the need to pay up for top teams and will, in our view, continue to push deals higher to stand out from, or at least not fall behind, the competition.

Even so, transition packages at most traditional brokerage firms are formulaic, typically ranging from 150 percent to 350 percent of an advisor's trailing twelve-months (T12) production. There are outliers, however, and in today's market, it is not unusual to see deals north of 400 percent for the most elite advisors and teams.

Just as powerful for advisors considering change is the fact that deal structures are increasingly advisor-friendly. The most successful firms have tweaked recruiting deal structures. They may include provisions for unvested deferred compensation reimbursement. Some shift the economics to be more front loaded (where back-end bonus dollars are usually structured as non-guaranteed earnouts whereby an advisor must hit agreed upon asset or revenue hurdles to achieve the incentive). Some include the (previously unheard of) repayment of an advisor's outstanding financial obligations. There are even guaranteed all-cash deals. And, even more creative deal terms are doubtless coming.

While it's true that the lengths of forgivable notes attached to these deals have gotten longer, in some cases up to fourteen years (which most advisors view as a negative), our view is that advisors are always free agents so long as they spend any monies they receive only at the rate at which the note forgives. For example, an advisor tied to their firm by a nine-year note who wants out in five, must plan for the fact that they would need to pay back at the time of departure 4/9th of the monies received.

It is becoming more common for firms to offer twelve- or thirteen-year loans attached to recruiting packages, with the longer time frame serving as a way for them to justify more aggressive deals as they amortize the forgivable loans over a longer period of time. Exceptions do exist: If a team has an advisor who is looking to retire earlier than the note forgives, many firms are willing to customize deals to match that advisor's time horizon—as long as the firm will retain the assets upon the advisor's retirement.

As an example, here's a typical (hypothetical) transition deal for a team generating $3,000,000 in annual revenue:

- 300 percent total deal on a nine-year forgivable loan (representing $9,000,000 in total potential deal money).
- 150 percent cash up front ($4,500,000).
- 30 percent in stock to offset the loss of unvested deferred compensation ($900,000).
  Note: Many firms offer unvested deferred comp reimbursement in the form of cash with a cliff vesting period attached.
- 50 percent cash bonus paid if 80 percent of the assets move within the first six months ($1,500,000).
- 70 percent in cash bonuses spread out over five years based on asset portability and growth (in this example, an advisor would need to exceed 150 percent of their recruited assets within their first five years to attain the full headline 300 percent deal) ($2,100,000).

There are other ways in which advisors maintain leverage when being recruited, particularly in this strong seller's market. It's reasonable and increasingly common for advisors to negotiate increased compensation for staff salaries, hefty travel and entertainment budgets, and the payment of other local expenses, along with negotiating the headline transition package.

## What Makes an Attractive Business?

The reality is that the wealth management industry has always operated on a basis in which larger advisors and teams fetch the highest deals. And that certainly remains true today. That said, a few other characteristics may make an advisor's business more or less attractive, influencing deal economics. These factors include:

- Percent advisory versus commission-based revenue; firms prefer fee-based business over commission business.
- Potential for portability and genesis of client relationships; firms look more favorably on self-generated business than revenue generated from firm referrals because of concerns about the portability of assets that have a higher likelihood of stickiness to a firm.
- The nature of products and services that make up the book; some products such as assets tied to proprietary models, alternative investments, and private transactions are, by design, not portable.
- Client demographics and concentration risk; firms may be concerned about an aging book of clients and

concentration risk, such as one large client that makes up 50 percent of the asset base.

- Number of client households; firms consider books of business with a smaller number of client relationships (preferably high-net-worth) more easily portable and, hence, more valuable.

- Growth trajectory; every firm would much prefer to recruit an advisor generating greater revenue from a continually growing small base of clients than one who is doing more business but whose growth is stagnant.

All that said, in the end, this is a human business. Recruiters and managers are more inclined to go to bat for people they view as good cultural fits; almost every firm has a "no jerks" policy when recruiting advisors. Although deals are largely formulaic, there is a subjective element to every single one.

> Although recruiting deals are largely formulaic, there is a subjective element to every single one.

One final note on transition deals: Bigger firms typically have less flexibility on deal structures and terms relative to their boutique counterparts.

In the wirehouse world, advisors can anticipate payouts ranging from 40 percent to 52 percent of revenue generated. However, the cash payout may be considerably less since many firms (notably the wirehouses) defer between 5 percent and 15 percent of an advisor's total compensation as a way of binding their advisors to the firm. Regional and boutique firms tend to offer similar payouts, though they often provide more in the way of cash compensation.

It's also possible that an advisor's true net payout ends up less than the stated headline number because large firms are typically willing to cover only certain expenses, often in a limited capacity. Advisors are commonly left to foot the bill for some or all additional expenses associated with running the business, including support staff salaries and bonuses, travel and entertainment, marketing, and discount sharing. So, when comparing your firm's comp to another's, be sure you are making an apples-to-apples comparison.

Compensation plans themselves are certainly a source of contention at many firms, but it's the *changing* of these plans that often frustrates advisors the most. The big brokerage firms alter these comp plans on an annual basis to incentivize (or penalize) certain behaviors or to cut costs. One of the reasons advisors increasingly flock to the regional and boutique firms is that they tend to keep compensation relatively simple and very rarely alter their plans.

## The Negotiation Process for Advisors at Wirehouse Firms

While advisors typically have little leverage at their current firm, there is significant leverage in being recruited. And the more substantial your book of business, the more leverage you will have. You can use this leverage to obtain a better deal, added incentives like money for travel and entertainment, additional sales support to be paid for by the firm, bigger office space, a better office location (sometimes a firm might even be willing to open a new office for you if you generate enough production), payment of automated customer account transfer (ACAT) fees, or an increased marketing budget.

But remain aware of this important reality: Firms typically aren't into playing games. The opening bid is usually close to the top offer. That said, there is almost always room to negotiate around the margins. When a firm presents a deal to you, we recommend the following:

- Don't negotiate piecemeal. Know what your final asks are and go back all at once.
- Go into this process knowing full well that it's unlikely you will get 100 percent of what you asked for. So don't start negotiating until you are sure what you will accept if the firm comes back with a counteroffer.
- It's bad form to ask a firm to negotiate against itself without being willing to commit. With a commitment in hand, you will have the most leverage in asking for a better deal. Plus, the person presenting the offer could be your next colleague or boss, so you want to begin the relationship on the right foot. If you take nothing else from this chapter, let it be this: The willingness to commit is the most powerful leverage there is.
- Don't play games or even think about going back on your word. Negotiate in good faith and only with the firm you are willing to commit to.
- Understand what is reasonable before negotiating so as not to overshoot or offend the firm making the offer.

When a firm presents an offer, it's perfectly reasonable to ask for time to process and digest it. There's no need to commit to a firm on the spot. In fact, it's advisable to take some time to assess the offer—but not so much time as to make the firm wonder if you are really serious.

And this is a crucial piece of advice: Keep deal terms *confidential*—it doesn't serve you or the firm to brag about it.

For those who have never seen competitive recruiting offers before, it can be difficult to evaluate what constitutes a good or fair offer. Ultimately, a good offer is one that you feel provides requisite value relative to the risk and disruption you are sure to endure. On a more practical level, most advisors put far more weight on the up-front deal portion of the deal relative to any back-end earnouts because the up-front portion is more guaranteed. I think it's important not to dismiss back-end bonuses because they can be quite meaningful. If you are an advisor in growth mode, you would do well to bet on yourself.

To ensure that a move will make sense from a financial perspective for you, ask yourself:

- How much unvested deferred compensation (if any) would I leave on the table if I were to move?
- How much money would I owe back to my firm if I were to leave before any remaining contractual obligations (for example, remaining money left on a prior recruiting deal or money owed from a sunset deal or retiring advisor program) were fully forgiven?
- Would I stand to lose a future successor opportunity (the ability to take over a retiring advisor's business)?
- Would I leave any portion of my business behind, either because it couldn't be serviced at a new firm or because some assets are locked into non-portable positions?

- What are my personal financial goals? Will this move impede those goals or enable me to reach them faster?

If there are back-end hurdles to be met in a transition deal you are evaluating, assess how likely you are to hit them. While almost every advisor prefers a more front-loaded deal, don't dismiss the power that growth can have on the ability to achieve a back-end bonus.

One final word of advice: Don't assume that the deal your advisor friend got will be the same as what you might be offered. While it's true that many components of a deal are formulaic, every advisor's value to a firm is different; and deals, along with the recruiting appetites of firms, may vary over time.

## Transition Deals in the Independent Space

As we described in chapter two, independence in the wealth management industry is not a one-size-fits-all model. It is a catchall term that describes various types of affiliations and setups, ranging from independent broker dealers to RIAs. Within the various models of independence, there are meaningful differences in the levels of transition support, ongoing operational support, compliance oversight, and other attributes. For the purposes of this chapter, we will focus on the economics.

> The real draw of independence comes from superior take-home pay, the equity that one is building, and the ability to create real competition for the business and sell it to the highest bidder.

Let's make one core fact clear: Transition deals in the independent space are not in the same ballpark as deals in the wirehouse space. And it's unfair to compare the two, since even the lowest paying brokerage firms offer more than the most aggressive independent options. That said, some versions of independence do indeed come with an expectation of transition cash. We will dive deeper into the various models below, but the overarching theme is that the more independent you are, the less transition money you can expect to receive. The real draw of independence comes from superior take-home pay, the equity that one is building, and the ability to create real competition for the business and sell it to the highest bidder at aggressive multiples when ready, with long-term capital gains treatment.

Starting with the independent broker dealer model, which is widely regarded as the most restrictive flavor of independence, these firms commonly offer transition packages between 30 percent and 100 percent of an advisor's trailing twelve-month's production (T12) or gross dealer concession (GDC), as of the time of this writing. There are a few notable outliers that pay north of 100 percent. The forgivable notes attached to these deals range from five to ten years, depending upon the firm and size of package. While most often the deals are paid up front, some broker dealers build in back-end bonuses to balance their risk.

By comparison, in its purest form, the RIA space comes with no explicit transition dollars. The do-it-yourselfer who works with a custodian (like Schwab, Fidelity, Pershing, or most recently, Goldman Sachs) to establish their own RIA firm will likely receive business development incentive dollars (sometimes referred to as soft dollars) from the custodian to defray start-up costs and pay some direct expenses, but these sums are not intended as a means to monetize one's business. For such advisors looking to capitalize the business in a more meaningful way, alternative options to unlock liquidity include bank loans, minority and majority equity investors, and acquirers.

There is one other version of independence worth discussing as it has become arguably the hottest segment of the landscape in the past decade: the supported independent space. These models offer advisors the look and feel of the do-it-yourself RIA space, but without many of the headaches that advisors dislike about building and operating an RIA. Namely, they provide transition support and ongoing middle- and back-office support, and sometimes compliance oversight as well. Such firms charge a revenue override for utilizing their platforms, but they occasionally offer transition capital for advisors who affiliate with them. Transition dollars, when offered, are typically comparable to what independent broker dealers offer, approximately 40 percent of an advisor's annual production.

So why would an advisor choose to go independent when the short-term transition economics are so much less than what they might receive from a traditional brokerage firm?

It's because the real win in independence comes from being just that: independent. That means a few important things from a day-to-day perspective. Certainly, it means more autonomy over your business life relative to being an employee at a traditional firm. It also means better take-home economics (a well-run independent firm can reasonably expect to net around 65 percent of revenue). Plus, advisors have control over operating margins and the ability to greatly expand them by adding inorganic growth to the revenue mix via mergers, acquisitions, or recruiting, while keeping fixed costs like rent and staff salaries relatively static.

This concept of retaining operating leverage, in which each incremental dollar of revenue adds to the bottom line as fixed costs remain consistent, is a powerful motivator for independent business owners. By contrast, when you are an employee, that benefit belongs entirely to the firm you work for.

For the advisor who is willing to be long-term greedy, there's tremendous potential to building an enterprise, the value of which can ultimately dwarf even the most aggressive recruiting deal from a traditional firm. It is this ability to build equity in your own business—equity that one day can be sold for a significant multiple (see below)—that advisors find so compelling about the independent space.

On the topic of selling an independent business, there are a few important considerations. First, a sale of a business is largely taxed at long-term capital gains rates, rather than the ordinary income classification associated with a traditional recruitment deal. And second, the business owner has complete control over who to sell to (whether that be a private equity firm, family office, local RIA firm, or even a bank), how many bids to entertain, and how and when to execute a transaction.

Independent businesses typically garner valuations of a multiple of earnings before interest, taxes, depreciation, and amortization (EBITDA) or free cash flow. Similar to traditional recruiting deals, valuations for independent businesses are near a high point as of this writing, with far more demand from buyers than supply from sellers. No one can predict future valuations, but advisors who bet on themselves and opt to build their own businesses are likely to reap the rewards at the end of the day.

The topic of business valuations is complex and highly customized, and there is much more to say on the subject. My partner, Louis Diamond, president of Diamond Consultants, and I coauthored an article for *Forbes* comparing three real-world scenarios that illustrate the potential that can result from building an independent business,[6] an updated excerpt of which is included here:

> Let's consider a wirehouse team generating $5,000,000 in annual revenue, managing $600,000,000 in almost all fee-based assets for high-net-worth clients. This team's desire for greater freedom and control over economics has made it very interested in going independent. Let's further assume that, as an independent business, the team's local expenses (including rent, staff costs, benefits, marketing and the like) would be 30 percent of annual

6   Mindy Diamond and Louis Diamond, "What's the 'Real' Value of a Financial Advisor's Business," Diamond Consultants, August 2020, updated May 2023, https://www.diamond-consultants.com/whats-the-real-value-of-a-financial-advisors-business/.

revenue and that an additional 30 percent of revenue would be allocated to advisor compensation.

In simpler terms, that would mean this $5,000,000 business would be left with $2,000,000 in EBITDA that would then be distributed to the owners of the business. If the business in its current state—with zero growth over a five-year period (a highly unlikely scenario)—were to be sold, it would be valued at $18,000,000 (assuming a 9x market rate multiple for a business of this size).

But, what if we assume that this $5,000,000 team grows at a compound annual growth rate (CAGR) of 10 percent for a five-year period? How does that impact the value of the enterprise? It more than doubles its EBITDA and enhances the multiple to a conservative 11x instead of 9x—thus doubling the value of the business overall.

## Figure 2. Base Case: No Growth for Five Years

| Annual revenue—year five | $5,000,000 | Equivalent to T12 production |
|---|---|---|
| Less: expenses | $1,500,000 | Estimated at 30 percent of revenue for a business of this size |
| Less: advisor compensation | $1,500,000 | Estimated at 30 percent of revenue to cover advisor compensation |
| EBITDA/cash flow available to owner(s) | $2,000,000 | |
| EBITDA multiple | 9x | Estimated market rate multiple for a business of this scale |
| Estimated valuation | $18,000,000 | EBITDA multiple*EBITDA |

## Figure 3. Organic Growth Alone: 10 Percent CAGR for Five Years

| Annual revenue—year five | $8,052,550 | Equivalent to T12 production |
|---|---|---|
| Less: expenses | $2,013,138 | Estimated at 25 percent of revenue for a business of this size |
| Less: advisor compensation | $2,415,765 | Estimated at 30 percent of revenue to cover advisor compensation |
| EBITDA/cash flow available to owner(s) | $3,623,647 | |
| EBITDA multiple | 11x | Estimated market rate multiple for a business of this scale |
| **Estimated valuation** | **$39,860,117** | EBITDA multiple*EBITDA |

And, finally, let's look at how the same compound annual growth rate of 10 percent for five years, plus the acquisition of a $2,000,000 practice in year five, impacts overall enterprise value. A conservative 12x multiple is now applied to EBITDA because the scale of the business has increased—and that yields a valuation of well over $50,000,000.

**Figure 4. Organic Growth and Acquisition: 10 Percent CAGR for Five Years and $2,000,000 Acquisition in Year Five**

| | | |
|---|---|---|
| Annual revenue—year five | $8,052,550 | Equivalent to T12 production |
| *Plus:* acquired revenue | $2,000,000 | |
| Combined annual revenue—year five | $10,052,550 | |
| *Less:* expenses | $2,513,138 | Estimated at 25 percent of revenue for a business of this size |
| *Less:* advisor compensation | $3,015,765 | Estimated at 30 percent of revenue to cover advisor compensation |
| EBITDA/cash flow available to owner(s) | $4,523,647 | |
| EBITDA multiple | 12x | Estimated market rate multiple for a business of this scale |
| **Estimated valuation** | **$54,283,764** | EBITDA multiple*EBITDA |

Unpacking this a bit: Most often, independent-minded advisors break away from the traditional brokerage world because they are frustrated—hamstrung by limitations and bureaucracy and burdened by the loss of control. Yet, they are also driven by a desire to accelerate growth (and retain a greater percentage of revenue) and to add inorganic growth to the mix by way of recruiting and M&A.

As figure four above illustrates, the operating leverage and margin expansion that is achieved by moderate organic growth plus a $2,000,000 acquisition serves to greatly expand the value of the business overall—by almost 3x!

So, the answer to the most frequently asked question, "How can it make sense to go independent where there's no up-front money, when I can get a 300-percent-plus deal from another major firm or opt in to my firm's retiring advisor program?" lies in these illustrations.

Despite the fact that an independent business can garner much greater enterprise value at the end of the day than one that sits under a traditional brokerage firm umbrella, for many advisors, independence is just a bridge too far. It requires more start-up work than they desire and a long-term view that may not be practical. The good news is that as the industry landscape has expanded, there are many boutique and quasi-independent options that give advisors the support, scaffolding, and additional control and freedom they seek, plus a handsome transition package and much of the upside that rewards growth on the back end. Very often, we meet advisors who tell us they are certain that they want to be entrepreneurs and start their own firms, but when they walk through the diligence process and discover all that goes into doing so, they find they much prefer a middle-ground solution.

## What to Think About When It's Time to Decide

A winning negotiation brings together two motivated parties: The advisor/business owner who has determined that a prospective acquiring firm is the right one, and a firm that believes this advisor's business is a good fit for it. Put another way, the more each wants the other, the more likely the right deal will be struck with the appropriate mix of cash up front and back-end incentive bonuses.

Likewise, motivation equals flexibility when it comes to negotiating the terms of a deal: The more motivated you are, the more flexible you are likely to be. That said, you need to be comfortable with walking away from any deal that's not the right one—that is, one that doesn't address your top priorities. It's exceedingly rare to get *everything* you want in a deal, which makes it critical to have clarity on your needs, goals, and ultimate reasons for considering the change. Deals get done when both parties are willing to compromise.

This usually isn't a one-and-done process. Most advisors will create a bidding process for their business and consider multiple offers—typically no more than three—from firms that are at the top of their list. Additionally, by soliciting multiple offers, advisors can often gain leverage and a positive impact on deal structures.

Referring to the answers you provided on the self-assessment in chapter three, pay careful attention to your goals and the gaps you are looking to close. Then ask:

- How close does each firm come to helping me achieve my goals?
- Does one firm meet the criteria of "better enough" more than another?

Be sure to compare each prospective firm against one another, as well as to your current situation if you opted not to sell.

Ultimately, you shouldn't consider putting yourself, your support staff, and your clients through the disruption of a move, merger, or sale unless you are certain that any prospective new firm can bring demonstrable valuable resources to the table and offer you a better quality of life. This is another time when it's important to remind yourself that no matter how attractive a deal's terms might be, if a prospective buyer can't solve for what you are currently missing, then it isn't the right deal.

> # The first rule of thumb when it comes to making any change: *Do no harm to clients.*

It is also important to remember the first rule of thumb when it comes to making any change: *Do no harm to clients.* So, make sure that a new firm allows you to do everything you are currently doing for clients and then some. While there will likely be some clients for whom this new firm is not right, be sure you consider the impact on your business as a whole:

- How would I feel if those clients didn't follow me?
- Alternatively, how would I feel if I opted not to consider a new firm because it didn't meet the needs of just a few clients?
- Do the limited needs of a select few clients justify passing up an opportunity that might be accretive for everyone else?

## Additional Considerations for Independent Business Owners

Client needs, and the ability to service them, are certainly an important factor for anyone considering a potential transaction. Beyond that, though, an independent business owner considering a sale or merger needs to be laser-focused on the additional benefits that an acquirer might bring to the table, such as some or all of the following:

- **Improved technology.** Do they have a state-of-the-art open architecture tech stack?
- **Better service.** When something is broken, who fixes it?
- **Value-added services.** Does the deal include additional M&A opportunities and expertise, trust and estate advisory, tax advisory, business and growth coaching, or anything else that could potentially move the needle?
- **Succession planning.** Does a transaction solve for succession for you and your firm?
- **Compliance.** Does a transaction take compliance off your plate? Will compliance be business-friendly under the new firm umbrella?
- **Freedom and flexibility.** Will you lose all connection to the firm you built if you sell? Does the buyer allow autonomy over investments, marketing, and client prospecting, for example? What about day-to-day policies like remote work?
- **Scale.** Does the new firm help you compete better in a crowded landscape? Are they big enough to have already solved for what might be missing from your firm? Are they too big? Will you lose culture and the ability to get things done quickly?

Often, the decision about whether to sell comes down to the desire to monetize all or part of the business and the comfort with ceding control. Some buyers require conformity while others will allow relative day-to-day autonomy. And while clearly selling all or some of your business means ceding some control, there can be real benefits to a transaction.

The conversation around selling all or a part of an independent business is one we often have with guests on our podcast. I recommend an episode with Michael Nathanson, the CEO and chair of The Colony Group,[7] as a great starting point on the value of taking on a capital partner (though there are many other episodes in our podcast series that speak to this topic as well).

## Recap

The key to a successful transition is to make sure that a new firm allows you to do everything you are currently doing for clients and more—and that you will be able to make a strong case to clients in support of your choice. Ultimately, no matter how big the financial incentive, you shouldn't put yourself, your team, and your clients through the disruption of a move unless you are confident that a new firm is more than better enough in terms of all or most of the things you are looking to solve for and the quality of life it can offer you.

While deals are largely formulaic, each is customized to the unique potential value an advisor brings to a firm. Most often, advisors have limited, if any, leverage with their current firm—but there is leverage in being recruited. And the more substantial your book of business is, the more leverage you will have.

---

7   The Diamond Podcast for Financial Advisors (formerly Mindy Diamond on Independence), "20X Growth in 10 Years: A $20B RIA on Embracing the Value of Private Equity and Interdependence," Diamond Consultants, February 2023, https://www.diamond-consultants.com/20x-growth-in-10-years-a-20b-ria-on-embracing-the-value-of-private-equity-and-interdependence/.

When it comes to negotiations, firms typically aren't into playing games. While their opening bid is usually close to the top, there is almost always some wiggle room for negotiations.

Evaluating a new firm or opportunity should be about the confluence between bettering your ability to serve clients and accelerating the growth of your business. Only after that, should you take your personal financial well-being into account.

# Chapter Seven

# Getting It Right: Thinking of Your Business as a Business

Over the past decade, the shift in advisor mindset has served as one of the greatest drivers of change in both advisors' lives and the industry as a whole. And while we've talked about many of these changes, perhaps the one most worthy of further discussion is the notion of advisors thinking of their business *as a business*.

Regardless of whether they practice as employees or independent business owners, the best advisors are looking beyond the short term, and evaluating whether their firm allows them the opportunity to build their business the right way for the long term.

It's a mindset that develops as advisors recognize that the practice they built (regardless of whether they practice as independents or employees) has immense value that they can monetize now and in the future. If a firm no longer serves their needs, advisors have greater options and more confidence in portability with clients who, in most cases, are more loyal to them than to the firms at which they work.

The escalation in client demands also drives this evolved advisor mindset, increasing the importance of differentiation to fend off fee compression and commoditization. Plus, the industry landscape has evolved to offer a greater array of options than ever before, making it possible for advisors to have more freedom, control, and agency over their professional lives without sacrificing anything, including enhanced client service.

This is one of the main reasons that advisors bristle so much when their firms announce new mandates and restrictions: It can feel as though the firms are inserting their authority more and more into sacred space—the advisor's business.

Ultimately, advisors are responsible for asking the tough questions of themselves and the firms they work for to ensure they are indeed in the right place to serve their clients and grow their businesses with the greatest level of autonomy and control.

This chapter looks at several important concepts and strategies that advisors should think about when evaluating the status quo.

## Imagine Forward

Take the time to envision what a more perfect future might look like and ask yourself the tough questions to identify whether where you are now will enable you to reach your desired destiny.

Put another way, take the opportunity to "imagine forward" —a concept related to the second habit from Stephen R. Covey's *The 7 Habits of Highly Effective People*.[8] That is, "begin with the end in mind."

---

[8] Stephen R. Covey, Jim Collins, et al., *The 7 Habits of Highly Effective People: 30th Anniversary Edition (The Covey Habits Series)*, Simon & Schuster, October 2020.

Picture what you would like your ideal business to look like at the end of the day and ask yourself the following:

- Am I achieving all I want to?
- Is my firm a help or hindrance?
- If I had a magic wand, what changes would I make to my business?
- If I could hit the easy button to get from here to there, where would "there" be?
- What additional support do I need?
- Do I aspire to build an enterprise? Do I want to be a business owner?
- What things don't I know that I wish I did?
- How do I want to live my business life?

Once you've answered these questions, then it's about doing a gap analysis between where you are and where you want to be, assessing the gap, and determining if any action is required.

This is not a sales pitch to suggest that you make a move. On the contrary. It's an exercise we encourage advisors to conduct on a regular basis—whether they are entertaining change or not—and to use what they've learned to take action to achieve their desired goals.

## Client Relationships and Portability

After spending a professional lifetime building and nurturing relationships, the last thing an advisor wants is to lose ground—especially since the motivation for any move should be to improve client service and accelerate growth. That's why many advisors who are considering change often lie awake at night asking themselves some of these questions that we first raised in the previous chapter:

- Will my clients follow me?
- How deep are my relationships?
- Do I have the confidence to test their loyalty?
- Do I want *all* of my clients to follow, or is this a good time to do some purging?

How should someone in exploration mode attempt to predict client portability? Here are steps that I suggest you start with:

## Assess the Depth of Your Client Relationships

- What is the genesis of each client relationship? Did you bring the client to your current firm, or did you inherit the relationship? Self-generated relationships are more likely to be portable. Plus, inherited relationships may fall outside of Protocol protection or carry with them stricter non-solicitation mandates.
- Are you the clients' sole point of contact at the firm? Are there others who interact closely with them? Keep in mind that if those who are closely involved choose to stay behind, the more vulnerable you are to losing those relationships if you make a move.
- What is the nature of your client relationships? Do you provide all-encompassing guidance, or are you relied upon strictly for investment management? Do your clients use other advisors to manage different aspects

of their financial lives? The depth and scope of each relationship will have an impact on portability.

- Have you moved previously, and, if so, how recently? While a client may be forgiving of one transition, each ensuing move creates an opportunity for them to reassess your value, thereby increasing the potential for client fatigue and loss of the relationship.
- Have you asked yourself, "What's in it for them?" While doing no harm should serve as your true north in a move, you must be certain that things will be better for your clients at a new firm and that your reason for moving is clearly to their benefit.

## Assess Your Book of Business

- Which assets are invested in proprietary products that cannot be held elsewhere? If there is a percentage of your book that is not portable, determine if there are options at a new firm that will work for your clients and yield similar results. Will the change trigger unfavorable tax consequences? Are there other negatives to moving clients out of one investment and into another?
- Are there assets held in illiquid vehicles (such as private equity, real estate, etc.) that cannot move due to lock-up periods or other restrictions? Determine if those clients would still move with you despite some of their assets being left behind.
- What third-party managers are most critical to your business? Are the same managers on the new firm's platform? If they aren't, can they be added or otherwise accessed? As no two platforms will ever be identical,

you'll need to understand the process for adding necessary third-party providers to the new firm's platform—and if there is even an appetite to do so.

- To what extent do you leverage your firm's credit, lending, and banking capabilities? Determine whether a new firm will offer the support to replicate and service these needs. And, how are these services accessed: in-house or through third-party institutions?
- Do you service any "sticky" clients such as firm executives, corporate stock plans, and institutional accounts? Any of those may be less inclined to transition for a myriad of reasons.

After you assess your business overall and determine which assets and clients are portable, you have one final question to answer: Is the potential of a move still greater than what you might leave behind?

## Shrink to Grow

Letting go of assets is not easy for anyone to do—emotionally or financially—because advisors are conditioned to focus on asset growth above all else. And in a world where bigger is considered better, why would the Street's most talented and productive lot opt to go against the grain?

It comes down to clarity of vision and the determination to remove any and all barriers to achieve it.

With almost every advisor I've represented or counseled, I've asked them to imagine a world where they leave some assets behind: either because they are indeed not portable (for example, proprietary products or alternatives that are locked up via a feeder fund) or because they are taking a more strategic viewpoint and choosing to do so. For the latter, it typically means leaving behind a certain type of business like institutional or international relationships or lower-asset clients who may not fit a more current ideal profile. While there are some advisors who report 100 percent of their clients transitioning shortly after their move, it's important to determine what *your* comfort level is. For example, would you be satisfied if only 70 percent to 80 percent of your clients followed?

This is a concept I call "shrink to grow"—a strategic decision to take a step backward to create a new foundation that will allow you to take many steps forward.

Advisors who take this route are those who determine the following:

- They are serving a segment of clients that is no longer profitable or is too time-consuming relative to the amount of revenue it generates.
- They are managing a large asset base but generating a concomitantly smaller percentage of revenue from certain assets.
- They are tired of serving clients who are unappreciative or toxic.
- They want to eliminate commission-based business and focus exclusively on advisory revenue to move into a more fiduciary model.
- They want to take their business upstream and serve a smaller number of larger clients or reinvent their ideal client profile.
- They want to go deeper with a smaller number of select households.

Making the decision to shrink to grow isn't only in the purview of those who are thinking about change; it's good business hygiene for all advisors. It's about being strategic in your decision-making.

Ultimately, if you've decided that a move is in order because it's best for your business and clients overall, don't allow a few relationships to hold you hostage.

> If you've decided that a move is in order, don't allow a few relationships to hold you hostage.

## Partnerships

Speaking of relationships, there's great value in building strong partnerships and teams. The synergy of compatible skill sets and expertise creates a foundation for what could be a long and happy marriage, with the benefit of adding scale, capacity, and a built-in plan for succession.

To be sure, firms strongly encourage their advisors to form ensemble practices because it works to the firms' advantage: It means that clients will receive a more well-rounded experience, and at the same time it makes the assets stickier and harder to move.

But, like a marriage, sometimes the shared mindset that partners start out with may not remain consistent over time. Each individual may ultimately want different things as they grow, for example, how they expand their team, how they service clients, how they divide responsibilities, and how they think about succession. As partners evaluate stay versus go, these evaluations often illuminate these differences. This common inflection point can leave partners wondering if they are better together or apart.

So how do you determine that? Here are six questions that can help you decide how best to move forward.

1. **Are you still compatible with one another?**
   The passage of time can deteriorate the bond of even long-term partnerships rooted in friendship. You need to decide if the value of the relationship contributes positively to the value of the business.

2. **Do you share similar goals and vision?**
   This is one area where we see partners become quickly divided, particularly when they may have been part of an arranged marriage where they were united at the direction of their firm, instead of one where like-minded people came together of their own choosing. So, regardless of the genesis of your partnership, it's critical to ensure that you are aligned on all aspects of your business, including planning for the future, how you service clients, growth, risk tolerance, and succession.

3. **Are you better together—better able to serve clients, manage your team, and grow?**
   The most successful partnerships often act more like a basketball team than a bowling team. Players should have specific roles to magnify each other's strengths and cover more ground, grow faster, and serve clients more efficiently. It should feel more like 1+1=3, rather than separate in-

dividuals who may be serving clients separately and not as a cohesive unit.

4. **If you are different ages, are you on the same page about succession plans?**

   From the senior advisor's perspective, it's important to be comfortable with the next-generation inheritors who will replace you and lead the business into the future. Likewise, if you are in line to succeed a senior partner, you need to be unified on how and when that partner will step away and transition the business to you, as well as the impact that the senior partner's retirement will have on your options, take-home economy, and long-term enterprise value. (More on this topic below.)

5. **Are you in agreement with respect to making a move?**

   If partners are not aligned in terms of the level of satisfaction with their firm, that can fray even the strongest relationships. Likewise, in a situation where partners agree on their dissatisfaction, they may not agree on their willingness to do something about it.

6. **And, if you were to consider a move, do you agree on which type of firm or model you would go to?**

   Partners need to be aligned on what they see as the right next option for their business—one that supports like-minded short- and long-term goals. When partners don't see eye to eye on whether the next step for the business is to leave for another traditional firm or go independent, for example, one partner would need to compromise. They may opt to stay put by default or go their separate ways.

It's certainly not easy to separate from someone with whom you've worked for years, which is why many opt for the path of least resistance, staying together as long as the benefits of doing so outweigh the potential downside. But, sometimes those differences become too big to ignore.

For more on the topic, download our Partner's Quiz worksheet available on the resources page (https://www. diamond-consultants.com/book-resources/).

## Succession

Succession planning has become one of the hottest topics in the industry and a leading driver of advisor movement. Cerulli's study "The Impending Succession Cliff" reports that more than one-third of advisors are expected to retire within ten years, setting up the transition of nearly 40 percent of assets. Yet 26 percent of advisors still do not have a succession plan in place.[9]

While the lack of a plan is often attributed to short-sightedness by advisors, the real issue is a scarcity of next-generation talent available to succeed those set to retire.

Advisors have invested a lifetime building a business with real value, but they can only realize that value if they have a next-gen successor in place who can ensure continuity, not only sustaining but also growing the business into the future.

The dilemma for many top advisors who do not have a next-gen successor in place is determining if an appropriate successor exists within their current firm and local market.

---

[9] "The Impending Succession Cliff," Cerulli Associates, March 2023, https://image.marketing. cerulli.com/lib/fe3411737164047c7d1072/m/1/4be6c8c1-0a2f-4922-9787-0206b7e8b1aa.pdf.

When they cannot find the right match, soon-to-retire advisors often opt to explore options elsewhere as a way of multiplying the potential number of suitors for their business.

Yet even those advisors who have a next-gen successor wrestle with the notion of how they will ultimately monetize their life's work. As a result, most wealth management firms have developed programs—such as Merrill's Client Transition Program (CTP), Morgan Stanley's Former Advisor Program (FAP), UBS's Aspiring Legacy Financial Advisor (ALFA) Program, and Wells Fargo's Summit—that allow senior advisors to retire in place and the next-gen successors to take on ownership of the business over time.

For those advisors who are certain that their firm will be the right legacy for their business, their clients, and next-gen successor, these retire-in-place programs are a gift. They offer a path of least resistance, rewarding senior advisors for their loyalty and next-gen inheritors with a way to take ownership of a much larger business, despite the fact that they are buying an asset that they won't ultimately own because those assets belong to the firm. There are considerations that many advisors are not aware of as they contemplate the next steps in their careers.

Senior advisors need to be crystal clear about the contracts that bind them, fully understanding the agreements they are signing, specifically including any and all post-employment restrictions, because, ultimately, they are signing over their business lives to the firm.

> Whether you are the soon-to-retire advisor or the next-gen inheritor, it is imperative to be thoughtful and deliberate before you sign a succession agreement.

For the next-gen successor, as attractive as the opportunity may be to buy or inherit a book, these programs serve as powerful retention vehicles, binding the inheritors to their firms for a period of five years or more. Should these inheritors have their sights set on changing firms or models prior to satisfying the terms of the agreement, they may find a transition to be more difficult and costly.

The message here, whether you are the soon-to-retire advisor or the next-gen inheritor, is that it is imperative to be thoughtful and deliberate before you sign a succession agreement that will tie you and your business to your firm. Be 100 percent certain that you can live with any changes that may come down the pike during the life of the agreement. Know your options, because to sign away optionality means losing control of your destiny, and your destiny should be only yours to control.

That said, for those who choose not to sign on, there are other succession pathways to consider:

1.  **Go independent.**
    This is a path that often appeals to next-gen talent who are attracted to the notion of becoming entrepreneurs without ties to a corporate entity.

A senior advisor may be fortunate enough to have a next-gen partner willing to do the heavy lift that a move to independence requires. This would necessitate crafting a custom succession plan that identifies exactly when and how the senior advisor might retire. It provides the highest level of control, as opposed to the one-size-fits-all structure prescribed by a big firm's retiring advisor program. For example, some senior advisors may wish to stay with the business but step into a non-client-facing role, such as executive chairman, as a way of staying connected to the business with a greater level of flexibility. Determining exactly how an advisor wishes to retire or phase out is strictly up to the advisor and their next-gen team.

Plus, for those with their sights set on the longer term, independence is a way of unlocking the true value of a business. An independent business can put itself up for bid on the open market to a limitless pool of buyers, ranging from other independent firms to private-equity-backed platforms, family offices, banks, insurance companies, and many other types of strategic acquirers. This amplifies the enterprise value for both the senior advisor and the next-gen successor with multiple competing bids driving up valuation. In addition, this option enables unlimited creativity and flexibility around deal structure.

For a data-driven case study on how a multigenerational team created its own sunset agreement as an independent while offering superior economics (at long-term capital gains) to the retiring advisor and enhanced cash flow for the next-generation advisor, you can reference an article

Louis Diamond published in partnership with the CFO of Dynasty Financial Partners, Justin Weinkle.[10]

## 2. Move once, monetize twice.

Longer-tenured advisors who are feeling that their firm may not be the right partner for the long term, yet still want to stay in the game for at least the next five to ten years, may opt to move once and monetize twice.[11] That is, they can monetize the business in the short term by taking advantage of a significant recruiting deal, and monetize again when they retire via the new firm's sunset program or selling to another practice within their broker dealer.

This can be a lucrative and effective way of continuing to leverage the all-under-one-roof resources of a major firm, while not losing the opportunity to take meaningful chips off the table. However, I do not recommend this strategy if the motivation is simply to squeeze as much liquidity out of your business as possible. But, if you're considering a move because it will allow you to meet your goals and better serve clients, and it has the ancillary benefit of allowing you to monetize twice, then that can be a real home run.

## 3. Customize your own succession agreement.

There is one more path that we are seeing with greater frequency—one in which senior advisors identify a family member or other trusted next-gen advisor to succeed them.

---

[10] Louis Diamond and Justin Weinkle, "Multi-Generational Teams at a Crossroads: Wirehouse Sunset Program or Independence?", Diamond Consultants, September 2019, https://www.diamond-consultants.com/multi-generational-teams-at-a-crossroads-wirehouse-sunset-program-or-independence/.

[11] Mindy Diamond, "Move Once, Monetize Twice," Diamond Consultants, January 2019, https://www.diamond-consultants.com/move-monetize-twice/.

If collectively they decide that their firm's retire-in-place program is too restrictive, they can engage legal counsel to craft a custom agreement, separate and apart from the firm, outlining the parameters around the partnership, including the senior advisor's retirement process and the next-gen successor's purchase of the business.

This makes the senior advisor's retirement less prescribed and more of a personal agreement between the parties involved by taking their firm out of the equation.

## Non-Protocol Moves

Most every advisor who works for a wealth management firm has signed an employment agreement that specifies the post-employment restrictions that govern their behavior in a move. But when a move is covered by the Protocol for Broker Recruiting (as I discussed in chapter two) where both the advisor's departing and receiving firms are signatories to the agreement, the Protocol trumps non-solicit clauses in the advisor's agreement, so long as the advisor who is making the move adheres to all Protocol directives.

There's no doubt that moves made with Protocol protection come with the least amount of risk. Yet advisors make non-Protocol moves every day, as talented attorneys and the firms looking to recruit have their own playbooks on how to navigate these transitions. Even advisors with the most restrictive employment agreements—those that call for garden leave (in which an advisor would need to cease contact with clients for a prespecified period of time, sometimes up to three months) and noncompete clauses (where an advisor is prohibited from working with any clients that came from the firm they are departing from)—continue to move successfully.

Ultimately, if you are certain that you are making a move for the right reasons—reasons that are in the best interests of clients and the business overall—you can succeed with realistic expectations and the sage advice of legal counsel.

## How to Avoid Murphy's Law

Even with the best of planning, things can go wrong. That potential multiplies when advisors rush through the due diligence and transition planning processes. The good news is that you can avoid common mistakes if you take the time to be thoughtful and strategic.

In guiding countless advisors and teams through their transitions, we identified seven reasons why a move could take an unexpected wrong turn.

1. **Not going deep enough or asking the right questions during the due diligence process.**
   The due diligence process is, by definition, the time for you to be particularly thorough and detailed, asking every question about a prospective new firm and discovering how every aspect and nuance of your business would be supported. For example, many wirehouse advisors use their firm's discretionary model portfolios, but a new firm may not have similar solutions available. Or, a miscommunication between a new firm and the advisor about a particular holding that has the potential to affect many clients in their book could make transition a nightmare. This is the time to avoid assumptions about what can be replicated: The

onus falls upon the advisor to ensure that a new firm is fully aware of every detail of their business.

2. **Not going deep enough when vetting the financial stability of a prospective firm.**
The banking crisis of 2023 was a harsh reminder that advisors need to demand reverse due diligence on a prospective firm's financials. How well capitalized is it? How likely is it to withstand any storms? Are you comfortable with the firm's management structure? These are all questions an advisor should ask and have answered. Ultimately, there's no guarantee that you'll uncover all unforeseen problems, but you will come away with a better understanding of the firm's risk management profile.

3. **Overestimating client loyalty and portability.**
In most cases, clients are loyal to their advisors and not the firms they work for. But any advisor considering change must be rigorously self-aware and make sure that they have always done right by their clients and acted as the best possible steward for them. This is the best way to realistically assess the likelihood of portability. Advisors who have moved before must be able to give airtight reasons to clients for choosing to change jerseys again.

Ultimately, the single biggest determinant of client portability is delivering a strong "what's in it for them" message. That assures all parties concerned that an advisor is moving not for their own financial gain but rather for the clients' benefit. If there isn't a strong enough upside for the clients, there's a greater risk of losing them.

Outside of client loyalty, the ability to replicate what the advisor is currently doing for their clients will determine who can and will follow. For example, is the advisor confident that their alternative investments (alts) business will port over? What are the lockups associated with each position? Would a client follow their advisor to a new firm if part of their assets couldn't move for a year or more? Could you live with that? What about clients' outstanding loan balances? Can the rates and terms be matched without penalty? Would clients move if doing so would cost them money? In any case, it's imperative to be clear how a move would still be worthwhile—even if it meant losing some business at the outset.

4. **Relying on a handshake or verbal promise.**
Certainly, there are plenty of oral agreements made during the negotiation process, and, no doubt, it's easy to get caught up in the moment. But advisors must memorialize a verbal promise or handshake from senior management or a branch manager of a prospective new firm in a memo of understanding (MOU) to avoid land mines down the road.

5. **Not meeting senior leadership.**
To fully ensure that an advisor's goals, sensibilities, and vision are congruent with that of a prospective firm, I recommend requesting time with its senior leadership. This is an opportunity to ask questions about the firm as it stands today and its perspective for the longer term—and confirm that the firm's answers align with yours.

6. **Overestimating your partners' and support staff's loyalty.**
   Having honest and transparent communication—and listening carefully—is vital to understanding if everyone on the team is aligned. Are all equally committed to the same ideals, or do the partners have different perspectives regarding how they want to grow their business and where they want to spend the next decade? If there is a disconnect, what would it mean if one left and the others stayed? What about feedback from the staff? What kind of future are they looking for, and can you provide it to them after the move? How will their lives be made better by making a move? Knowing this and effectively communicating before a move is critical to creating a smooth transition for each member of the team. But keep in mind that Protocol prohibits an advisor from pre-soliciting their staff, so proceed with caution, following the advice of counsel as to what you can say and when.

7. **Knowingly or unknowingly violating post-employment restrictions or the Protocol.**
   An advisor's move is either governed by the post-employment restrictions outlined in their employment agreement or, where applicable, by the Protocol. Violating non-solicit provisions, taking proprietary documents, or soliciting team members to join the advisor at a new firm are all actions that can result in a legal mess. Plus, deliberately poking the bear and not leaving on good terms can cause the firm left behind to be vindictive. The number one best practice is to work with an attorney who is knowledgeable and experienced with advisor transitions and explicitly follow their advice.

## Recap

The best advisors are looking beyond the short term and evaluating what goes into growing a successful business for the long term—and whether their firm can support all they want to achieve.

Thinking of your business *as a business*, there are some important concepts and strategies you might consider:

- **Imagine forward.** Begin with the end in mind and picture what you want your ideal business to look like at the end of the day.
- **Client relationships and portability.** Evaluate the depth of your relationships and the ways you can continue to add value to both your clients and your business.
- **Shrink to grow.** Identify whether you have created the right foundation that will allow you to take many steps forward with those who fit the ideal client profile, even if it means jettisoning some assets.
- **Partnerships.** Assess whether you and your partners are better served together or apart.
- **Succession.** Whether you are a soon-to-retire advisor or next-gen inheritor, consider all options before you sign a retire-in-place agreement that will bind you and your business to the firm.
- **Non-Protocol moves.** While moves made with the Protocol protection come with the least amount of risk, non-Protocol moves are successfully accomplished every day with guidance from legal counsel.

- **How to avoid Murphy's Law.** Even with the best of planning, things can go wrong. And, that potential increases exponentially when advisors rush through the due diligence and transition planning processes. Fortunately, taking time up front to strategically plan your transition will help you avoid common pitfalls.

Evaluating your business life means examining every possible aspect of it to ensure that you are indeed in the best place to serve clients and grow your business with the greatest level of autonomy and control. If you determine that a move is warranted, you must consider every facet with acute self-awareness and a strategic plan designed to lay a foundation to achieve the goals you've set both for the short and long term.

# Chapter Eight

# Do You Stay or Do You Go?

As I think about the wealth management business as it was a decade ago, it's hard not to recognize the major shift in advisor mindset.

What was once a focus on the short term (Who's paying the top deal?), has morphed into a big-picture, long-term view. Advisors, especially the top teams, are thinking of their businesses as businesses, placing greater value on freedom and control. They ask:

- Who will succeed me and how will the business live beyond me?
- Will my goals and values continue to be congruent with my firm?
- How can I protect and maximize the value of the business I've built?

This point of view has become a powerful driver of movement, because while the status quo may be good enough for today, it may not be for tomorrow. Combined with an industry landscape that now offers bountiful possibilities, advisors have a significantly greater likelihood of finding a better option.

And this is the crucial decision point.

Because the fact that you're reading this book indicates that you at least have questions about how well your current firm is serving you, whether there is a better option, or if you can tap your untapped entrepreneurial spirit to serve clients in a different, and better, way.

That is, "good enough" may no longer be acceptable.

Over the past seven chapters, I introduced you to the evolved landscape to give you a sense of what's out there and what the due diligence process looks like.

More importantly, you took time to get introspective and answered the tough questions about your business life. You assessed your current firm, identifying any gaps that may exist in your ability to serve clients and grow your business. And, hopefully, you learned plenty about yourself and gave serious thought to what actions you are willing to take to achieve your best business life in the process.

Through due diligence, you may have identified one or more opportunities that were intriguing. But—and this is critical—you should only be willing to disrupt your business if one of those options was more than better enough. And this is where the value of being flexible comes in. Because as we said earlier in this book, nothing in life is perfect. So you'll need to be clear about what your list of uncompromisable must-haves are, how important it is to achieve them, and how ready you are to accept that not every one of your boxes will be checked.

Armed with knowledge of your personal reality, you're well-equipped with the clarity needed to conduct the ultimate test: the compare-and-contrast exercise. It's the final assessment you need to perform before you pass go (or stay, as it might be) and the criteria that will help you decide what comes next.

The final challenge is to answer this: How does your current firm measure up to other firms or models you might be considering? And have you seen an option that might better serve you, your clients, and your business?

The burden of proof now rests on the other firm or model: It must prove to be not just slightly better, but more than better enough to warrant the risk and hassle of making a move. If the other options are only slightly better, then the tie goes to your current firm.

If that's the case, this may have led you to the conclusion that you're happy enough where you are and need not take the exercise further. That's great, because it verifies that you are in the best place for your clients and your business. You can move forward from a position of strength, knowing full well that you are fulfilling your fiduciary obligation.

Or perhaps you have found an option that's more than better enough. Then you must ask yourself: Do you have the energy, the desire, and risk appetite to actually do something about it?

Because not everyone does. Change is hard—so it really needs to be worth it.

You might be wondering why I'm trying to talk you out of making a move. And that's a fair question.

When I started in the recruiting world decades ago, I realized something: My role is to serve as a guide. To give you the education and tools you need to make an informed decision, help you ask the tough questions, then share possibilities based on your answers. And, then to trust that only you know what's ultimately best for you and your clients.

Only you can answer the question that you started out with on this journey:

"Should I stay or should I go?"

No matter what your decision, my wish is that it leads you to your best business life.

# Afterword

### by Louis Diamond
President, Diamond Consultants

It was 1998 when Diamond Consultants was born. At that time, my mother, Mindy, didn't expect it to become one of the top financial advisor recruiting and consulting firms in the country.

Yet here we are, more than two decades later, Mindy presiding as CEO of a firm that she started (literally) on the bedroom floor of our home.

Mindy's professional journey began in 1984, when she graduated from The George Washington University with a degree in accounting. Her first job out of college at a New York City Big Eight public accounting firm quickly revealed that she was a people-person trapped in a world of numbers and spreadsheets.

Three years into her accounting career, Mindy answered an unsolicited call from a recruiter at an executive search firm pitching various accounting jobs in the industry.

During a conversation, the recruiter—who also noticed Mindy's passion for people over numbers—asked Mindy what would become a life-changing question:

"Do you find the work you are doing to be satisfying and soulful?"

As someone who came from a family that always followed the straightest path, the one of least resistance, Mindy assumed that her degree dictated her direction—and despite how unhappy she really was with her career choice, she would never have considered abandoning her defined path.

Yet the fundamental question that the recruiter asked Mindy intrigued her in a way that she couldn't ignore. What came next was the real game changer—an offer for her to become a recruiter with that search firm.

My father, Howard, always Mindy's biggest champion, encouraged her to take a leap far outside of her comfort zone and accept the offer.

And that she did. Mindy worked for the recruiting firm for seven years, thriving in a world where she felt rewarded both personally and professionally. Year after year, as the top recruiter among hundreds of her peers, she guided others to find their own ideal career paths—setting the early stages for a mindset that would later drive the mission of the yet unborn Diamond Consultants.

Mindy describes her early tenure as a recruiter: "I never thought of myself as working. I just loved that I was helping others find a position that better suited them when it was appropriate, one that might be more exciting and fulfilling."

As much as Mindy loved the work she was doing, thankfully for my brother Jason and me, she put her career on hold for several years to be a stay-at-home mom. But as we grew up and time passed, she felt an itch to get back into the game.

As Mindy tells it, in the summer of 1998, at dinner with friends Ed Friedman (then branch manager of Morgan Stanley's Ridgewood, New Jersey, office) and his wife Julie, the conversation turned to the lack of capable recruiters in the wealth management field.

And by dessert, ideas flowed around a business plan for what would soon become Diamond Consultants.

By September, Mindy started the business on her bedroom floor with nothing but a pad, pen, telephone, and a sense of reluctant determination.

Though Mindy's previous recruiting experience was in a world that was highly transactional—one where the goal was to sell a prospect on a specific role or job opportunity—it was a notion she was increasingly uncomfortable with.

Instead, her desire and natural ability to connect with people, understand their motivations and goals, act as an objective consultant instead of a salesperson, and help them gain greater agency over their lives served as Mindy's true north.

And it was through this work that her impact yielded positive and measurable results.

Those results became evident in the earliest days of Diamond Consultants, where her natural instincts were to change the way recruiters traditionally worked with advisors.

Mindy opted to always make it about the advisor first.

Mindy began every conversation by asking advisors the same life-changing question that she was asked years before. But she took it a step further, challenging everyone to question the status quo and the value they derived from it. She empowered them through education to step out of their comfort zone and not be satisfied with the path of least resistance if it did not serve them best. And she also reminded them that staying put was perfectly acceptable if that was in their best interests.

Mindy's way of life is to look at each person as an individual with unique goals: Real people, not just clients, and definitely not transactions—or, as she puts it, "It's always about what's best for the advisor, and it's never about my personal financial gain."

Mindy nurtured this advisor-first approach over time, and it serves as the foundation for Diamond Consultants' success. And as a result, the firm has grown through several office locations and on to our current headquarters in Morristown, New Jersey.

## The Next-Generation Perspective

You might say I literally grew up in the business, earning a degree in finance and international business from Mindy's alma mater, The George Washington University, and later working in the financial services field at Morgan Stanley, UBS, and Ernst & Young.

Like Mindy, my experience at those firms laid an extraordinary foundation for the work I do today. But I, too, was looking to make a more tangible impact on the lives of the people I served. And frankly, deep down, I had an entrepreneurial itch to satisfy.

It seemed only natural that someday I would join Mindy in the pursuit of expanding upon the mission she created decades ago—a mission I watched grow over the years and saw as the right next step in finding my own best business life.

While our staff has grown over time, now including my brother Jason, our team members have become family, too—many having joined early on and remaining with us to this day.

Yet none of us, including Mindy, are ready to rest on the laurels of our success. And just like the advisors we work with, we're always looking to grow and expand our reach to do more for others.

Our success over the years serves as a testament to the strength of our mission and the core values that guide us:

- To educate the wealth management community, sharing our knowledge, intel, and experience you may not be otherwise privy to, without expectation or commitment.
- To be trusted partners to our advisor-clients, serving as objective guides with a singular focus on their needs.
- To encourage advisors to think deeply and strategically, putting aside emotion so they can make smart, informed decisions.
- To do all this with the ultimate goal of guiding advisors to achieve the best results—financially, professionally, and personally.

I'm proud to represent a firm that has grown literally through perseverance in the pursuit of fulfilling one's true potential. And I'm honored to help Mindy—my mother and partner—build a legacy poised to live on for generations. But mostly, I'm grateful that I, too, am living my best business life.

And it's our goal to help you do the same.

If after reading this book you feel inspired to indulge your curiosity, we encourage you to reach out to us. We're happy to have a conversation without obligation or expectation, and always in the strictest of confidence.

Here's to living *your* best business life!

# Appendix

## Resources

The tools and resources mentioned in this book are available for download via the QR code below or at https://www.diamond-consultants.com/book-resources/.

Barbara Herman, "Surviving Due Diligence: 10 Tips for Financial Advisors," Diamond Consultants, January 2020, https://www.diamond-consultants.com/guide-surviving-due-diligence-process/.

Mindy Diamond and Louis Diamond, "What's the 'Real' Value of a Financial Advisor's Business," Diamond Consultants, August 2020, https://www.diamond-consultants.com/whats-the-real-value-of-a-financial-advisors-business/.

The Diamond Podcast for Financial Advisors (formerly Mindy Diamond on Independence), "20X Growth in 10 Years: A $20B RIA on Embracing the Value of Private Equity and Interdependence," Diamond Consultants, February 2023, https://www.diamond-consultants.com/20x-growth-in-10-years-a-20b-ria-on-embracing-the-value-of-private-equity-and-interdependence/.

Louis Diamond and Justin Weinkle, "Multi-Generational Teams at a Crossroads: Wirehouse Sunset Program or Independence?", Diamond Consultants, September 2019, https://www.diamond-consultants.com/multi-generational-teams-at-a-crossroads-wirehouse-sunset-program-or-independence/.

Mindy Diamond, "Move Once, Monetize Twice," Diamond Consultants, January 2019, https://www.diamond-consultants.com/move-monetize-twice/.

"The Diamond Podcast for Financial Advisors (formerly Mindy Diamond on Independence)" podcast, https://www.diamond-consultants.com/podcast-mindy-diamond-independence-2/.

"Perspectives Articles Library," Diamond Consultants, https://www.diamond-consultants.com/category/articles/.